FACING SUFFERING
a Christian response

Herbert M. Carson

FACING SUFFERING

a Christian response

EVANGELICAL PRESS

EVANGELICAL PRESS
P.O. Box 5, Welwyn, Hertfordshire AL6 9NU, England

© Evangelical Press 1978
First published June 1978

ISBN 0 85234 119 9

Cover design Peter Wagstaff

Printed in Great Britain by
Stanley L. Hunt (Printers) Ltd., Rushden, Northamptonshire

CONTENTS

PART I   THE PROBLEM IN GENERAL

  1   WHY DOES GOD ALLOW IT?   11
  2   TOWARDS AN ANSWER   15
  3   BIBLICAL CASE HISTORY (1): JOB   21

PART II   PRACTICAL ANSWERS

  4   YOUR FATHER CARES   31
  5   THE SYMPATHETIC CHRIST   38
  6   THE HOLY GHOST THE COMFORTER   45
  7   FINDING A PURPOSE IN PAIN   53
  8   BIBLICAL CASE HISTORY (2): PAUL   61

PART III PARTICULAR APPLICATIONS

  9   BEREAVEMENT   71
 10   MENTAL AND PHYSICAL HANDICAP   79
 11   UNHAPPY MARRIAGE   86
 12   DEPRESSION   96
 13   WALKING IN THE DARK   111
 14   BIBLICAL CASE HISTORY (3): JEREMIAH   118
 15   TO SUM UP!   125

To the people of God at St. Michael's, Blackheath, St. Paul's Cambridge and Hamilton Road Baptist Church, Bangor, where I learned many of the lessons of this book.

PART I

The Problem in General

God moves in a mysterious way
  His wonders to perform;
He plants His footsteps in the sea,
  And rides upon the storm.

Deep in unfathomable mines
  Of never-failing skill,
He treasures up His bright designs,
  And works His sovereign will.

W. Cowper

CHAPTER 1

WHY DOES GOD ALLOW IT?

"Man is born to trouble as the sparks fly upwards." One of Job's comforters was certainly right at that point, even though he was wide of the mark in much of his other comment on suffering humanity. Pain and suffering are the inevitable accompaniments of being a man. They are the common condition of all men everywhere. There are no exceptions here. To be human is to face the issue of suffering.

Our suffering is due in the first place to our mortality. We are all of us born to die! From the moment we draw our first breath life is a losing battle against the ageing process which sooner or later ends in death. Modern medicine has made enormous strides in prolonging life so that the expectation of life in Western Europe is much higher than a generation ago, and vastly higher than that of under-developed countries. But medical care is at best a stay of execution. Inevitably we all die.

Moreover, death is not a simple transition from one sphere to another. It is closely linked with pain. Often its arrival is preceded by diseases of varying degrees of painfulness. Sometimes it comes by accident or by violence, when the pain is felt by those left behind to face the crushing shock of a sudden bereavement. Death inevitably means for most of us pain and tears and the sorrows of shattered lives.

Apart from our innate mortality there is the further factor of our environment which can at times be hostile. The monsoon fails in India and is followed by the grim aftermath of famine. A tornado rips through a countryside and leaves a trail of destruction and misery. Even the most sophisticated societies, with their ability to control nature in many of its aspects, reel helplessly under the terrifying impact of an earthquake.

Then there is the heart-break of young parents looking at their child in his physical or mental handicap. Instead of the promise of a full life there is the bleak prospect of an existence which, in its most extreme form, scarcely seems to touch the level of what we would think of as human life. Add to all this the misery which arises from man's inhumanity; the children born with diseased bodies because of their parents' loose living; the sad wreckage in hospital wards as the result of drunken driving; the pathetic victims of violent crime and of that supreme example of man's brutality to his fellows – war.

In all this there is a major factor which makes man's suffering more intense than animal suffering. He is able to anticipate pain. He discovers he has some incurable disease, but he also knows of others who have suffered intensely from this malady and he can easily deduce what his own prospects are. This anticipation of pain and the mental anguish, which can accompany the actual pain when it comes, are both accentuated by the desire for life and health. A man wants to live; his instinct of self-preservation is strongly developed, yet he knows that he is going to die.

But there are further acute problems which arise when we begin to reflect on suffering. For one thing, the degree of suffering often seems to bear no relation to the quality of the sufferer's life. A ruthless criminal evades the law and enjoys a healthy life in luxurious surroundings, while a district nurse is injured in a car accident and spends the rest of her days almost totally paralysed. To the onlooker it seems a cruel world, where justice has no bearing on what really happens.

Then again, there is a great inequality in the quota of suffering borne by different individuals. One person lives a long and healthy life with a happy family and a successful career. Another one faces debilitating illness, the loss of a child and the collapse of his career. I recall visiting a woman dying of cancer who had just had news that her husband had been killed in a tragic accident at work. Such, we say, is life; but we cannot shrug off the insistent questions which press in upon us: Why the inequity of suffering? Why does this family bear the brunt while others are comparatively unscathed? Why does one country enjoy reasonable standards of life and security while another is devastated by floods?

If men in general have problems with suffering, the Christian has even greater problems. If other men ask "Why?" in face of pain, the Christian's "Why?" is often wrung out of deep agony of soul. It is in fact his faith which presents him with the problems, though paradoxically it is that same faith which furnishes him with the answers. He believes in a God who is good and who is also almighty. But if God is almighty, so the anguished argument runs, why does He permit men to hurt and destroy one another? If He is good then surely He will use His almighty power to avert the pains and miseries which are the blight of humanity. In stark terms the question is: "How can a God of love permit such things as mentally retarded children, famine-stricken populations, thousands dying in agony from a multitude of diseases, the horror of earthquakes or the slow lingering misery of starvation?"

If he were an atheist in a godless world, where he is just one more species struggling for survival, he would have no questions to ask; but then he would have no answers either. The human heart cries out for an answer which reaches down to the sorrowing and the sufferer with a word which brings some hope in a world of despair. The old Stoic philosophy of a grim unyielding despair in the face of the buffetings of fate may sound a noble ideal, but in fact it is a bleak cold message to a sensitive soul who cannot muster the resources of an iron will-power. It may sustain some, but it only sustains them in a numbed hopelessness.

At the other extreme from the Stoics in Greek philosophy were the Epicureans. They recognised that sickness and death were inevitable. They saw too that men, with their warm emotional life and delight in living, would not, in a majority of cases, be satisfied with a rigid, despairing call to brace themselves to face the worst. So the Epicurean urged that since you cannot do anything about death, the best course is to ignore it and extract as much enjoyment as you can from life as you meet it. "Eat drink and be merry for tomorrow we die."

Like every brand of escapism, however, this is a short-lived and futile remedy. The night of jollification is followed by the morning misery of a hang-over. And the ostrich-like attempt to bury the head in the sand of some diversion or other, is a counsel of despair. It does not avert the coming crisis and in fact, by trying constantly to run away from trouble, makes a man even more incapable of facing the trouble when it comes.

For some, the lofty heights of Stoic fatalism are beyond them and the Epicurean trough nauseates them, but they still have no answer. All they can do is relapse into a condition of self-pity; but of all the possible reactions this is one of the most futile. It does not help to answer the questions. It does not strengthen the sufferer to face the pain. In fact it is utterly counter-productive in that it leads to a sterile condition of bitterness and cynicism. And these after all are only a sad variation on the theme of despair which underlies the other reactions to the problem of suffering.

Has the Christian any more satisfying answers to the problem than others who have grappled with it? He believes he has, but one thing he tries to avoid is glibness. The glib talker always has an answer ready. Often it is a pat answer that he has acquired from others. Certainly it is superficial, for it fails to dig deeply and explore the real issues. But to be glib or superficial in face of someone else's suffering is to add pain to pain. To dismiss the problem easily when someone is crying out in anguished desperation for an answer is a callous insensitivity which the Christian should want at all costs to avoid.

Nevertheless, he must also admit that he does not have the final and complete answer. Answers there certainly are and they bring great comfort, but there are still areas of mystery. There are still unyielding problems to which his only response is "I don't understand, but thank God I can trust my heavenly Father". How true Paul's words are: "We know in part" (1 Co. 13: 12).

CHAPTER 2

TOWARDS AN ANSWER

We begin our attempt to answer the problem of pain by looking at some areas of suffering where the issue is reasonably clear. There is first of all the very wide field of suffering where man himself bears the responsibility, and can in no way blame his Creator. If a man is promiscuous and ends with a diseased body or with insanity, he himself is responsible. If by his greed he exploits the soil or pollutes the water supply or the atmosphere then it is not the God, who gave him the ground to till and the fresh air to breathe, who is at fault. If by excessive indulgence, either by gluttony or drunkenness, he ends in a premature grave, it is he himself who has done it.

However, there are allied areas of pain where at first sight the issues are not so plain. It is one thing to say that it is a man's own fault if he wrecks his own body, but what are we to say of the suffering which comes to others from his selfishness? The syphilitic may reap a grim harvest from his pleasures, but he may also inflict blindness on the child he brings into the world. The drunkard may destroy himself, but at the wheel of a car he may also maim or kill others. The prosperous factory owner who dumps cyanide or lets poisonous effluent into the sea is corrupting the enrivonment for others.

Our reply is a further question: "Is God to blame because He did not create robots to be controlled by some heavenly computer rather than men with moral responsibility, even though they have grossly abused their freedom?" Then also we must look more closely at the problem of the innocent sufferer, for all too often the "innocent" in one situation becomes himself the selfish exploiter in another. Thus the old days of colonialism were stained by the brutal exploitation

15

of men and women who toiled in virtual or actual slavery to enrich their European masters. But the departure of the imperialists and the independence of the enslaved have not altered the picture. Now it is people of the same-coloured skin who are the masters, but they are just as selfish as the old and as ready to exploit their fellows. So, too, the nineteenth-century exploitation of workers by ruthless bosses is succeeded by the self-centred attitude of the big labour battalions who care little for the small unions or the pensioners so long as they get their very large slice of the cake. Innocence, we discover, is often a relative term.

But this still leaves us with major problems. A natural disaster is clearly independent of human agency. The tornado, the volcano, the earthquake – these are not precipitated by man's activity, but they cause immense suffering. Then, again, there are the tragic accidents which are in no sense due to human wilfulness. It may be because of the mechanical failure in a car or it may be due to human frailty in the miscalculation by a pilot, but in these and innumerable similar cases men are surely not to be held personally culpable. The same is true in the birth of a handicapped child to a couple who may have been chaste before their marriage and have not contributed by their actions to the tragic and inexplicable condition of their child.

Our first approach to these great problems is to note one basic fact in the human situation, namely, the reality of the spiritual catastrophe described in Genesis 3 and which Christians refer to as "the Fall". This great act of disobedience by the parents of the race is set in the wider context of the rebellion of Satan and his angels against the supreme authority of God. Indeed the disobedience of Adam and Eve may be viewed as their capitulation to the Enemy, involving them not only in his rebellion but in its terrible consequences. Thus the Fall is an event of human history, and is also part of a moral catastrophe of cosmic proportions. It is not therefore surprising to discover the unending ramifications of the disaster.

There is, of course, the primary consequence, namely man's alienation from God, but from this condition so many sad consequences flow. To be in communion with God is to know the Creator and to know as a result, His gracious purposes for creation. So in Genesis 2 Adam shares with his Creator in the naming of the animals, and also in the appreciation of an environment which was not hostile, but friendly; indeed, in God's own words, it was "very

16

good". But, alienated from God, man's mind is darkened. He now knows neither God nor God's laws for himself and for the created order. Before, he has been told to replenish the earth and subdue it, but the subjection of nature for man's use requires a divinely-given wisdom. Left to the impoverished thinking of his fallen condition man can no longer control his own greed and so he exploits rather than subjects nature, and thus destroys both the earth around him and also himself and his fellows.

But man's rebellion also opened the door to the dominion of Satan. The fallen spirit who rebelled against the Lord became "the prince of this world". The world created by God was invaded by an alien force so that John can say "the whole world lies in the evil one" (1 Jn. 5: 19). Thus God, in His word of judgement in Eden, speaks of the enmity of Satan to the woman, an enmity seen supremely in his hostility to the Christ who was "born of a woman", but also to all the sons and daughters of Eve. This enmity lies behind so much of the misery and suffering which to us seem to be inexplicable.

That Satan is active in his malevolent work is seen in the book of Job, though it is reassuring to see that his dominion is still within the limits imposed by God. The Lord in His wisdom, and for reasons He has not disclosed to us, has allowed Satan a measure of dominion, but he is always subject to the supreme dominion of God. Yet even within these circumscribed limits Satan still wreaks havoc. So he is seen behind the loss of Job's family and property and behind the sickness and pain in Job's own body. In the same way Jesus speaks of the woman who was bent with some spinal disease as one "whom Satan bound for eighteen years". When Paul speaks of the exclusion of the offender from church fellowship as delivering him to Satan, it means he is subject to the activity of the devil who will destroy him physically (1 Co. 5: 5), though mercifully he cannot touch him spiritually. Once again we see the evil power which Satan wields. Paul himself knew that reality and spoke of his thorn in the flesh, whatever that affliction may have been, as "a messenger of Satan to harass me" (2 Co. 12: 7). However one interprets Revelation 20, one thing is quite clear; the loosing of Satan leads to the deceiving of the nations and to war (Rev. 20: 8).

So behind the lust and greed and cruelty of men which lead to the unending catalogue of suffering and misery there lies a darker shadow. There is a figure who lurks in the background, who deceives men into carrying out his purposes, and whose supreme ambition is to cause misery and unhappiness to men who, though fallen, still bear the hated image of their Creator.

But the word of solemn judgement in Eden not only spoke of the impairment of man and of the dominion of Satan; it also declared a curse on the ground, "Cursed is the ground because of you" (Ge. 3: 17). So even the created order has been deeply affected by the consequences of Satan's rebellion and Adam's sin. The world as we know it is not the harmonious structure which came fresh from the hand of God, and over which the refrain was repeated that "it was good". Instead there is a discord which has affected the fabric of creation, the functioning of nature, and the pattern of animal and human life. So we have savage and destructive elements in nature which manifest themselves in earthquake and flood. We have nature "red in tooth and claw" with one species preying upon another. We have malarial mosquitoes and disease-carrying germs. We have, in short, a creation in a state of deep discord, and the consequences of that discord reverberate in every corner of life.

The apostle Paul takes up this theme in the eighth chapter of his epistle to the Romans. He pictures the creation waiting with eager anticipation for the final glory, when not only will the people of God be perfected but creation will be renewed. So, he writes, "the creation was subjected to futility, not of its own will but by the will of Him who subjected it in hope". He declares his God-given hope for the created order that it "will be set free from its bondage to decay". But that day has not yet come. Meanwhile, like a woman in the intense pain of a labour unrelieved by modern anaesthetics, "the whole creation has been groaning in travail". The day of deliverance tarries and still it is the day of futility and pain, of decay and death.

If this were the end of the story it would be a prescription for unmitigated despair, but it is far from the final condition of things. The time of travail will end. There will be, in Peter's words, "new heavens and a new earth in which righteousness dwells" (2 Pe. 3: 13). It is the New Testament echo of the prophecy of Isaiah: "The wolf shall dwell with the lamb, and the leopard shall lie down with the kid, and the calf and the lion and the fatling together, and a little child shall lead them. The cow and the bear shall feed; their young shall lie down together, and the lion shall eat straw like the ox. The sucking child shall play on the hole of the asp, and the weaned child shall put his hand in the adder's den. They shall not hurt or destroy in all my holy mountain; for the earth shall be full

18

of the knowledge of the Lord as the waters cover the sea" (Is. 11: 6-9).

Admittedly this still leaves great questions unanswered. To say that the present discord in creation is the judgement of God, still means that the suffering and pain which flow from that discord flow ultimately from the eternal Judge. But then we must acknowledge that with our finite minds, and with minds also darkened by sin we cannot – and indeed we dare not – question the justice of the Almighty. Abraham's question still stands as a true affirmation of faith: "Shall not the Judge of all the earth do right?" (Ge. 18: 25). If this is God's sentence we must bow before His sovereign wisdom. We will learn in such submission to grasp in some small measure the infinite horror of sin which has wrought such havoc. We will learn also the wonder of God's answer to that sin, the redemption of Christ which will not only embrace all the elect of God but ultimately the universe.

But the judgement of God is not only to be seen in a general way in the discord of creation, but also in God's particular judgements upon nations and upon individuals. Here we need at once to counter a misunderstanding which is as old as the book of Job, namely that suffering is always a sign of special sinfulness and so of divine judgement. The disciples of Jesus also had this in mind when in the case of the blind man they asked if it was his sin or the sin of his parents which had caused his blindness. The unnamed questioners of Luke 13 had the same idea when they asked Jesus about the Galileans who had been massacred by Pilate.

In both cases Jesus is quite emphatic that particular sufferings do not prove the commission of particular sins. Of the blind man He says, "It was not that this man sinned, or his parents, but that the works of God might be made manifest in him" (Jn. 9: 3). On the Galilean massacre He replies with a question: "Do you think that these Galileans were worse sinners than all the other Galileans because they suffered thus? I tell you, No; but unless you repent you will all likewise perish" (Lu. 13: 3). We must not assume that because someone is suffering deeply it is a sign of God's judgement on him individually.

Yet having firmly registered this qualification, it must still be said that there are specific judgements for specific sins. Gehazi's leprosy was divine retribution for his covetousness and deceit. Ananias and Sapphira, whose sudden deaths are recorded in Acts

5: 1-11, are solemn reminders of the sinfulness of attempting to lie to the Spirit of God. In the history of the Jews as a nation there was the great crisis of the exile in the sixth century B.C. and the even greater catastrophe of Jerusalem's fall before the Roman soldiers in A.D. 70. In such national judgements the innocent suffer with the guilty. This was the agonising problem which faced Habakkuk, but he also had to learn what many another questioner has had to learn, that we in our limited wisdom must acknowledge our inability to grasp the purposes of God. "The Lord is in His holy temple; let all the earth keep silence before Him" (Hab. 2: 20).

There is however one other aspect of judgement which it is important to keep in view. It is the gracious purpose which God has in view when He sends the trial. Many a man who has persistently ignored the voice of conscience and the call of the gospel has been brought to his senses by pain or sorrow. C. S. Lewis put it very succinctly: "We can rest contentedly in our sins and in our stupidities. . . . But pain insists upon being attended to. God whispers to us in our pleasures, speaks in our conscience, but shouts in our pains: it is His megaphone to rouse a deaf world."[1] Long ago Hosea couched his call to repentance in the same vein, "Come let us return to the Lord; for He has torn, that He may heal us; He has stricken and He will bind us up" (Ho. 6: 1). There are many whose tragic reaction to suffering is bitterness and hatred of God. There are others who in the darkness of their tears see a light directing them to the celestial city. The light is God's mercy in the midst of His judgement and the response to that light is repentance.

[1] *The Problem of Pain*, p. 81.

CHAPTER 3

BIBLICAL CASE HISTORY (1)
JOB

"The patience of Job" – the phrase has become part of the English language, though many of those who use it to describe their needed patience in face of great provocation are describing suffering which does not begin to compare with his. He is one of the great sufferers of Scripture, and in the drama which bears his name the themes are worked out of human suffering and human sin, of man's folly and God's wisdom, of despair and hope. Whether in the stark simplicity of the prose passages or in the lofty sweep of the poetry which comprises most of the book, we are confronted with the basic problem of undeserved pain. In face of such suffering man will stumble in his uncertain attempts to find an answer. His solutions will not move beyond his own tentative groping. But from speculation to wisdom there is one sure way. It is summed up in the great conclusion: "The fear of the Lord, that is wisdom; and to depart from evil is understanding" (Jb. 28: 28).

The opening chapters not only set the scene for the great debate which is to follow, but also take us behind the scenes to see the powerful forces of evil which must be taken into account if we are to make sense of the suffering of the innocent. So we are introduced to the subtle and relentless activity of the Evil One. We are reminded that beyond the world we see, there is an invisible realm where spiritual forces are at work, whose influence upon the course of human history and of individual lives is beyond our full comprehension.

The evil spirit who plays a key role is designated Satan. The Hebrew word means "the adversary", and he appears here, as elsewhere in Scripture, as the enemy of God and of God's people.

The other titles which are used in the Bible refer to this basic enmity. He is "the Devil"; the Greek word diabolos means the slanderer. So in the garden of Eden he slanders God, as he persuades Eve that God's word is not to be taken at its face value and that God is no friend of those He has created. So here in the opening chapters of Job he slanders a truly godly man. In all the malicious charges which have been laid against the people of God down the years, and especially in the false accusations directed against Christ, we see the slanderous activity of the Devil. He is described in Revelation 12: 10 as "the accuser of the brethren" and the title there is supplemented by the other two titles, the Devil and Satan. In Matthew 12: 24 he is called Beelzebub. There is a variation in the manuscripts, some reading Beelzeboul. The two titles are closely related for Baal Zebub was a Philistine deity, the lord of flies; and whether by a change of spelling, or by a deliberate Hebrew comment on the alleged deity, the title became Baal Zebul, the lord of filth. In Matthew 12: 24 the further thought is present, that he is the lord of the demons. He himself is designated as "the demon" in Matthew 17: 18, for he shares the same nature with the other fallen spirits, but he is also their master and in his onslaughts on the people of God he has a powerful army of demonic auxiliaries.

He has access to God's presence. The precise mode of this access is outside our knowledge. What has been revealed is that, as a fallen angel, he has been cast out of heaven and reserved for judgement. Clearly then he cannot be sharing in the bliss of heaven, when the angels of God and the glorified saints join in adoring worship. The praise of heaven would have a note of discord if the twisted speech of Satan was part of it. The unsullied purity of the heavenly host would be tarnished by any contact with the "lord of filth" who is the very source of all the sin which has blighted mankind. Yet in some mysterious way he does have access to God. So "when the sons of God came to present themselves before the Lord . . . Satan came also among them" (Jb. 1: 6).

His reply to God's question about his activity indicates how widespread it is. He has come "from going to and fro in the earth, and from walking up and down in it" (1: 7). We do not need to conclude from this that Satan is either omniscient or omnipresent. These attributes belong only to God Almighty. But it does seem plain that he has a widespread activity, and as a disembodied spirit he may move with a rapidity beyond our ken. After all, if a man-made transmitter can flash a signal around the world, it is not difficult to envisage a devilish activity which moves far and wide. In addition to this he also has his demonic emissaries who are ready to do his bidding, and speed to run his errands.

To hear God challenging Satan is to have a further window opened on the problem of the suffering of the believer. The church of the living God is the great object lesson to the principalities and powers in the heavenly places (Ep. 3: 10). Each child of God is a trophy of God's grace, and every step he takes in a life of holiness is one more demonstration of what God can do with common clay. So God presents Job as a rebuke to the slanderer whose blasphemous aim is always to discredit the Almighty. "Hast thou considered my servant Job, that there is none like him in the earth" (1: 8). Here is a living repudiation of Satan's slanderous attacks on the integrity of God, for in Job God's sovereign grace is wonderfully exemplified.

But the slanderer is quick with his reply. Job has prospered mightily, so his religious profession has not hurt him in any way. But let God touch his possessions and, claims the Devil, Job will curse God to his face. It is at this point that we find not only the continuing mystery of God's dealings, but also a light of encouragement in the darkness. God permits Satan to do what he wants with Job so long as he does not touch him in person. Here are two encouraging truths in face of pain. In the first place Satan can only act by permission of God. The Lord does not stand back in helpless frustration. He takes the initiative with Satan, and He still retains it. God, not Satan, is the Lord of the universe. Then again, Satan's malevolence is held in check, and it is God who prescribes the boundaries beyond which Satan cannot go. That limit may seem at times to be beyond human endurance, but in fact the restraining hand of God is always there. Paul has the same thought as he writes to the Corinthians, "There hath no temptation taken you but such as is common to man: but God is faithful, who will not suffer you to be tempted above that ye are able; but will with the temptation also make a way of escape, that ye may be able to bear it" (1 Co. 10: 13).

Satan, when unleashed, acts with all the fury of an embittered adversary. Disasters fall like hammer blows. Job's children perish and his property is destroyed. There are human and material agencies involved. There are raiding Sabaeans and marauding Chaldeans. There is lightning flashing with destructive power, and a tornado spreading death and havoc. But behind these human factors and these natural calamities there is an evil power. We do well to remind ourselves that in this fallen world the pains and diseases, the suffering and the misery have often got an explanation which lies in a world beyond this one.

Job's initial reaction is magnificent. He might well have been overwhelmed by his grievous losses, but there is no hint of rebellion. The great slanderer does not succeed in enrolling Job as an agent to vilify the Almighty. Instead we find the quiet acquiescence of a man of God who has learnt to submit to the chastening of the Lord, and still to adore his God. Listen to Job and learn the right attitude to suffering: "Naked came I out of my mother's womb, and naked shall I return thither; the Lord gave, and the Lord hath taken away, blessed be the name of the Lord" (1: 21).

But the ultimate point in pain has not yet been reached. The Devil has been thwarted by the continuing godliness of Job. But there is further pain. The scene is re-enacted. Again Satan is challenged by God to consider the integrity of Job. Again the slanderer returns to the attack. This time his allegation is that Job is ready to forfeit everything to save his own skin. Let him taste pain in his own body and he will curse God, so Satan claims, and in response, God gives him a wider mandate. God is still in control for His permission is essential, and the limit on Satan's activity is still prescribed, but he is permitted to go further and to inflict physical pain so long as Job's life is spared.

We can draw two conclusions here about Satan's activities in the realm of suffering. In the first place he is able to bring sickness. He also has the power to cause death. The very fact that God imposes, as a restriction, that Job's life is to be spared, is an indication that but for that restraint the Devil could go further and end Job's life. But the statement that he has the power to inflict both illness and death must still be set firmly in the context of God's sovereign power. Satan may be permitted to act with destructive power but permission is required if he is to act at all, and the limits are clearly prescribed. God's ultimate aim is, of course, far removed from what Satan has in view. As the great adversary he plans only injury and loss, but the sovereign God has purposes in view which He will achieve through the Devil's malicious activity, namely, the blessing of His people and ultimately the manifestation of His own glory.

All this activity in the heavenly realm, however, is hidden from Job. All he knows is the further agony of intense physical pain as

24

his whole body is covered with sores. At that point we encounter two utterly diverse reactions. His wife responds with the angry bitterness which is the normal reaction of sinful men, "Curse God", she says, "and die". What is the point of life in face of such misery? This question is often asked, and tragically sometimes answered by suicide. But Job still shows his godliness as he submits to this fresh discipline from the Lord. "What? shall we receive good at the hand of God, and shall we not receive evil?" (2: 10).

It is now that the great debate begins. Job's three friends arrive. Eliphaz, Bildad and Zophar are clearly his friends; witness their intense shock at his wretched condition, and their obvious grief at his plight. Yet, as the speeches develop, it becomes increasingly clear that sympathy is not enough. Indeed sympathy without wisdom easily degenerates into censure, and advice which does not spring from the Word of God soon becomes blame. Certainly they say many things which are true, but their fundamental argument is false. Yet the very falsity of their various contributions is an important element in the total revelation. Like the black mounting of a jewel case which sets off the brilliance of the gems, so the erroneous theories of the three men simply act as a foil to enhance the glory of God's ultimate reply.

What then is their fundamental fallacy? It is one which continues through the three cycles of speeches, and is propounded with increasing severity. It is, quite simply, that great suffering implies great sinfulness. If Job has suffered so much, he must have sinned in some grievous way. Their view is that judgement on sin always happens in this world. If, then, a man suffers, it must be the judgement of God which he is facing. So Eliphaz puts it in terms of a question: "Who ever perished, being innocent? or where were the righteous cut off?" (4: 7).

The three friends emphasise great truths about God. Eliphaz stresses His moral perfection, Bildad His unwavering justice, and Zophar His omniscience. But of the grace and mercy of the Lord they know little, and of His wisdom which does not operate simply in the framework of this present world, they know nothing. As a result, each one surpasses the other in severity, until Zophar reaches the conclusion that Job has got less than he deserved. Throughout, the argument remains the same: suffering is God's judgement on sin, and the depth of a man's suffering is an index to the greatness of his sinfulness.

In face of the sustained barrage Job protests his integrity. There is no hidden sin of which he is guilty and for which he is suffering. Yet, under the pressure, Job begins to say things which later he bitterly regrets. He acknowledges the hand of God in it all, and rightly points to the fallacy in their arguments, for the wicked quite obviously prosper. But then another note creeps in. He feels desperately the remoteness of God – a feeling which often comes in times of great suffering – and his sense of God's irresistable power fills him with fear (23: 13-14). So he complains at God's apparent lack of concern in face of the injustice of the wicked (24: 1-12). God, he claims, pays no attention to the prayer of the sufferer (24: 12).

Yet in all the turmoil of soul, and even in the midst of his complaints against God, there are gleams of light which show the depths of true faith. The majesty of God makes him long for an umpire who might stand between them and plead Job's cause. Then, in a rare moment of insight, he speaks triumphantly of that need being met: "For I know that my redeemer liveth and that he shall stand at the latter day upon the earth. And though after my skin worms destroy this body yet in my flesh shall I see God, whom I shall see for myself and mine eyes shall behold, and not another" (19: 25-27). The whole book of Job is really a great cry of the heart to which the ultimate answer comes in the Person of the Redeemer Himself, who comes to save His people from their sins and to minister to them in their suffering.

There is one more important contribution to the debate before God replies. Elihu does not have the final answer, for that must come from God. Yet he has much to say that is profoundly true. Where Job's frustrated agony led the sufferer to irreverence, Elihu replies with a firm insistence on a reverent attitude before God (34: 10). God is the great teacher who instructs His people through the very bitterness of their pains (35: 11, 36: 22). One lesson, which even a godly man like Job still needs to learn, is the stubborn persistence of human pride; it is this pride which God humbles in the wretchedness of our suffering (33: 17, 36: 9). Suffering is not however a meaningless experience. It is a method of discipline which God employs for our ultimate benefit (33: 19). At such times God may seem to us to be in the remote distance, but the mediator provided by the Lord will bring the sufferer into the presence of the Lord. Here Elihu, like Job, is reaching out in hope to the coming deliverer. How much more can we look in confidence to the Saviour who has now come, and having accomplished His atoning work has become our all sufficient mediator and advocate.

Elihu ends his speech with an emphasis which anticipates the grandeur of God's own reply. Instead of trying to find our answers to the problem of pain within the narrow confines of our own little world, we need to lift our thoughts to God. The glory of creation about us displays on every hand the power and wisdom of the Creator. But while we can detect the edges of His ways, there is a depth of glory which we cannot plumb, and before which we must bow in adoring silence. "Behold, God is great, and we know him not, neither can the number of his years be searched out" (36: 26). "We cannot draw up our case because of darkness" (37: 19 R.S.V.). So until that day when "in my flesh I shall see God" there will be great and unresolved mysteries. Where we rebel against God's dealing we shall only flounder more miserably in the darkness. Where we learn to submit humbly to His providence, even when the way is very dark, we shall find the light of the presence of God illuminating the pathway ahead.

Elihu has prepared the way for the great finale of this majestic dramatic poem. God speaks, and before His word Job is brought low in penitence for the foolish words he has spoken. God's answer does not reply to many of Job's agonising questions, nor does it answer ours. God clearly will not be put in the dock to be cross questioned by His creatures. He will give answers, but they are freely given, and not because He wilts under the scrutiny of men. Indeed His reply follows a completely different line. It is to display the overwhelming majesty and greatness of God beside which man appears in all his puny weakness. The Lord ranges over the wonders of creation, and at every point man is the helpless onlooker. The pounding of the ocean and the light of the midday sun, the torrential rain and the ice gripping the surface of the lake, the quiet breezes and the flashing lightning, the complex life of the animal creation with the lion, the hippopotamus and the crocodile – all creation tells one great story. How great is our God and how worthy of praise and worship!

Set in the midst of God's sweeping survey of creation is an interjection in which He rebukes Job, and indeed all of us who are so ready to bring charges against the Lord. "Shall he that contendeth with the Almighty instruct Him? he that reproveth God, let him answer it" (40: 2). Job's immediate response to the rebuke is penitence. He does not capitulate to the charges of his friends who suggested that his righteousness was a pretence; and God Himself, in his later rebuke to the friends, will vindicate the integrity of Job. But godly man that he is, he yet knows that he has spoken foolishly. The valley of suffering can lead the most godly into cherishing false notions about God, and letting inner resentment fester until it issues in sinful words. But Job has learnt his lesson, a lesson that every suffering saint needs to learn. "Behold, I am vile; what shall I answer thee? I will lay mine hand upon my mouth" (40: 4).

It is in that attitude of humility and submission that he is able to listen with a deeper wonder to God's further words. As the glory of the Lord continues to unfold, so he abases himself before God; and in that self-abasement and submission he finds peace. "I have heard of thee by the hearing of the ear: but now mine eye seeth thee" (42: 5).

This book of Job furnishes various answers to the problem of the suffering of the righteous. The reply of the prologue is that it is a test of the genuineness of character of the man of God, and is one which demonstrates the grace of God to the watching world of spiritual powers. The answer of the three friends, that suffering implies personal sinfulness, is exposed for all its facile inadequacy. Elihu's contribution, by contrast, expresses the truth that suffering is a means of discipline in perfecting the saints in holiness. The ultimate solution however is found in the fresh revelation of the sovereignty of God. There will always be a profound mystery which it is beyond man's wisdom to penetrate, and the path of submission is the way to peace. But while suffering remains a mystery, we are not simply left with the thought of God as the majestic one beyond man's ken. He is also the gracious one who comes to the godly in his time of trial. It was not after his restoration to health and prosperity that Job found peace but while he was still in his physical wretchedness. He had not found all the answers, and indeed had come to see his own pride in his insistence that he must have answers. He has bowed in worship before the Almighty and has found himself, not like some Stoic submitting to a cold relentless fate, but like a child in the darkness gripped in his father's arms. The lesson was one which a suffering saint of the New Testament also learnt as he too listened to the voice of God: "My grace is sufficient for thee: for my strength is made perfect in weakness". Paul echoes the spirit of submission of Job as he replies, "Most gladly therefore will I rather glory in my infirmities, that the power of Christ may rest upon me" (2 Co. 12: 9).

PART II

Practical Answers

Ye fearful saints, fresh courage take!
  The clouds ye so much dread
Are big with mercy, and shall break
  In blessings on your head.

Judge not the Lord by feeble sense,
  But trust Him for His grace;
Behind a frowning providence
  He hides a smiling face.

W. Cowper

CHAPTER 4

YOUR FATHER CARES

When we discuss the problem of pain in a rather detached fashion we may content ourselves with general arguments and theoretical answers. When we are not personally involved in suffering it is rather easy to be dispassionate. But when suffering moves from being a topic for discussion to an actual experience then we begin to search much more insistently for an answer. The mind still requires answers which will throw some light on the problems, but as well as clarity of mind there is the need of the heart. There is a deep wounding of the spirit which requires not only a coherent answer which will explain, but an application of truths which will also heal.

We begin where the problem begins, with the character of God. It is this, as we have seen, which produces the problem of pain in the first place. If God is good and wise and all powerful, then how can He permit the pain and suffering which we meet everywhere? Paradoxically it is the very truths that pose the problem which also provide the answer. Struggling with our pain we need not only to see some of the factors which help towards an answer; we need, above all, a warm personal sympathy to help us in the hour of need – and that we find ultimately in God alone.

The basic starting point for the Christian is the revelation of God's character in the words and in the life of Jesus Christ. The title which came spontaneously to His lips and which He taught His disciples to use in prayer was "Father". But that title has been so robbed of its true glory by a sentimental approach that we have to eliminate the inadequate and erroneous notions which cling to it, before we can appreciate the wonder of the title "Father" and the implications for our own lives.

There is a vague notion, which is widely accepted, that God is Father in a completely unqualified way. This opinion is often presented in terms of questions. "Aren't all men children of God? Don't you believe in the brotherhood of man and the fatherhood of God?" To which the Bible gives a very firm reply, that the fatherhood of God is in fact qualified in very special ways. It is true that the title may be used in a very general sense to speak of God as the Creator, and thus as the source of life, but this universal fatherhood is at once qualified by the fact that men have rebelled against their Creator, so that Jesus can say, "You are of your father the devil". If men are to call God "Father", and if that title is to have any real meaning, then clearly there are important changes which must take place. To read such passages as these: "God is angry with the wicked every day" (Ps. 7: 11); "The wrath of God is revealed from heaven against all ungodliness and unrighteousness of men" (Ro. 1: 18); "Our God is a consuming fire" (He. 12: 29) – is to dismiss any shallow and sentimental views of a God who is not only perfect love but also infinite holiness.

In the Bible, the fatherhood of God is linked with His grace and His mercy. In spite of man's rebellion God has not abandoned humanity. He has reached into this rebel race with a mercy which men certainly do not deserve. He has revealed a gracious purpose: that of calling out a people who will be in a very rich sense His people, and for whom He will be their God. It is in the context of this new relationship between forgiven sinners and a pardoning God that God reveals Himself as Father. This obviously means that men cannot lightly lay claim to God's fatherly care. It is only when they have turned from their sins to seek the Lord, only when they have been reconciled to God, that they can turn to the Judge of all the earth and call Him "Father".

The key word in this issue is the one which the apostle Paul uses, namely, adoption. The sinner is outside God's family circle. Even there he enjoys God's goodness, for this gracious God "makes His sun to rise on the evil and on the good and sends rain on the just and on the unjust". He may pray, and God may in mercy answer his cry, but he has no rights, and no ground for expecting to be heard or claiming an answer. But when God has made him a new man, or, as Paul puts it, when he has become "a new creation" he is adopted into the family of God, and he can then say "Abba, Father".

Paul wrote as a Jew, with the background of an Aramaic-speaking family life. The title "Abba" was the affectionate and intimate title used within the home. But he also wrote as a citizen of Rome, whose legal system made adoption an irreversible act, so that the adopted child had an unassailable status in law. We can appreciate then why he is obviously so deeply moved when he writes to the Romans, "For you have not received the spirit of bondage again to fear; but you have received the Spirit of adoption whereby we cry, Abba, Father" (8: 15). Christ is, in a unique sense, the only-begotten Son of the Father. But the Spirit so unites sinners to Christ that they also are reckoned as sons, and have an immediate access to God Himself.

This great truth, which is so fully expounded by Paul, was already foreshadowed in the Old Testament. Listen to the psalmist: "Like as a father pitieth his children, so the Lord pitieth them that fear Him. For He knoweth our frame He remembereth that we are dust" (Ps. 103: 13-14). Among the exalted titles which Isaiah gives to the coming Messiah one of them is "the everlasting Father" (Is. 9: 6). So too Isaiah puts on the lips of the believer the confident words of trust: "Thou art our father" (Is. 63: 16, 64: 8). Jeremiah echoes the same theme when he brings God's word to the house of Judah: "Thou only shalt call Me, my Father, and shall not turn away from Me" (Je. 3: 19).

To the disciples, with their Old Testament background, it would not have come as a novel idea when Jesus told them to address God in prayer as "Our Father". What was new was that they saw this filial relationship in a unique way embodied in the person of Jesus. When He said "My Father", He spoke with an intimacy which clearly belonged to Him in a quite unusual way. But this only-begotten Son of God had been given by the Father to die for them. The purpose in view was that they should not perish but have everlasting life. And what is this eternal life? Jesus Himself gives the answer: "This is life eternal that they might know Thee the only true God, and Jesus Christ whom thou hast sent" (Jn. 17: 3).

To grasp this fundamental truth does not of course mean that all the problems are solved, and no painful mysteries remain. The boldness with which we come to God does not mean a glib familiarity, for the light which has revealed His truth to us has not conferred omniscience. There is much that we now know where formerly we were ignorant. There is much more which by God's grace we shall yet learn. But there is still a great deal of which we are and will continue to be ignorant. The position is well summed up in the book of Deuteronomy: "The secret things belong unto the Lord our God; but those things which are revealed belong unto us and to our children" (29: 29). There is an apt comment by Pascal concerning the truth of God in the Bible: "There is enough clarity to enlighten the elect and enough obscurity to humble them."

Here again the basic awareness of our relationship to God as Father helps us to understand why there is so much that is unexplained. When a child is small a parent will lay down rules without always being able to give a full explanation to the child. He insists that under no circumstances must the child accept a ride in a car offered by a stranger no matter how friendly the driver may be. To explain the reasons would be to introduce an undue element of fear and suspicion into the child's mind, so the parent has to issue what may seem to be an arbitrary edict. It may indeed appear like that to the child, but if there is a warm and trusting relationship the child will be ready to accept what he does not fully understand. He is prepared to trust his father and to accept that as he grows older he will be told more and will grasp more fully what is now rather obscure. So the Christian who knows God as his Father is content to await the full explanation which will be given in heaven. Meanwhile he studies all that God has revealed. He aims to find out as much as he can of what God has disclosed, but the secrets that remain do not produce resentment that he is left in the dark. He knows His Father and is grateful for all that has been revealed, but for the final answer he is prepared to wait.

It is not, however, all unresolved mysteries. There are "those things which are revealed", and they are ours to study and ours to enjoy. So we discover the further implications of the fatherhood of God, and what a message of comfort and hope they bring in times of perplexing suffering and bitter pain. We learn, in the first place, that our heavenly Father is all-knowing and all-wise. He is described by Paul as "the only wise God" (Ro. 16: 27). His wisdom is so deep that it leads Paul to burst into praise: "O the depth of the riches both of the wisdom and knowledge of God!" (Ro. 11: 33). Our Father is not looking towards an uncertain future and hastily improvising solutions as the pattern becomes clearer. That is the way men, with their finite minds, are compelled to operate, but the omniscient God knows the whole sweep of history and is majestically in control. So, where we cannot see one step ahead, and especially when the outlook

34

seems to be unrelieved darkness, we can turn in great confidence to the God who knows all things.

Thankfully we discover that our Father not only knows all things but that in a personal and individual way He knows us each one. He knows how our imagination reacts to the fears of a menacing future. He knows how the clouds of discouragement darken our horizon. Our temperament is known to Him. Our secret fears and pains are open to His sympathetic eyes. When we are in deep trouble we can be greatly helped by a sympathetic friend. But no matter how hard the friend may try to enter into our pain, he is always on the outside, for he is not able to probe the hidden recesses of our spirit. That is why suffering is so often an intensely lonely experience. But our heavenly Father is never the external sympathiser. He reads our hearts and so He can help and befriend us as no one else can. No wonder Job can still cling to an assurance in the midst of his pain. "But He knoweth the way that I take: when He hath tried me, I shall come forth as gold" (Jb. 23 : 10). The Psalmist has the same thought: "The Lord knows the way of the righteous" (1 : 6); "The eyes of the Lord are upon the righteous and His ears are open unto their cry" (Ps. 34 : 15). Jesus reinforces this confident trust as He assures His disciples, "Your heavenly Father knows" (Mt. 6 : 32).

The omniscience of God, if isolated from other truths, would be a terrifying thought. To think that our secret thoughts are naked and open to Him is by itself overwhelming. But this all-knowing God is also a loving God. He does not see as men see, for "man looks on the outward appearance but the Lord looks on the heart" (1 Sa. 16 : 7). He looks on His children, however, not with the scrutiny of the examiner, but with the tender concern of a loving Father, and with the sympathetic gentleness of One whose chief delight is our welfare. For proof of that love we return to Calvary. "God commends His love towards us in that while we were yet sinners Christ died for us" (Ro. 5 : 8). If God has gone to such extreme lengths as to give His own Son to such a death, then surely we have an unquestionable pledge that no matter how dark the hour may be, He will still care and will still provide. So Paul concludes with a confident question: "He that spared not His own Son but delivered Him up for us all, how shall He not with Him also freely give us all things?" (Ro. 8 : 32).

This does not mean that trouble will pass us by. In fact, to be unscathed in the battle of life would not be a proof of God's love, but of His unconcern. Hebrews 12 reminds us that "Whom the Lord loveth He chasteneth and scourgeth every son whom He receiveth" (12: 6). The argument is firmly presented. A father who loves his son will discipline him. An illegitimate child, of whom he is half ashamed, may well escape the punishment, for the father may find himself inhibited by his own guilty responsibility for the child's condition. So, says Hebrews 12 of those who are suffering God's chastening, "If ye be without chastisement of which all are partakers then are ye bastards and not sons" (v. 8).

The imagery used is significant, for He speaks not only of chastening but of scourging, that inexpressibly brutal punishment inflicted on a condemned criminal before crucifixion. So it is not some pin-prick which is in view, but quite overwhelming pain. Are we to say in such a moment of great suffering that God does not love and that He does not care? On the contrary, we are to see in the very pain a mirror which reflects the love of our God. He is more concerned with our character than our comfort. Because He is fitting us for glory hereafter, He is prepared to hurt us here. So the hand which inflicts the pain is one that is outstretched in mercy. Jesus' words to His disciples are unfailingly true, whatever the circumstances: "Your Father is merciful" (Lu. 6: 36).

But our heavenly Father's care is not only seen in His attitude towards us. He understands our needs and sympathises with us in our pains, but in addition to this He comes to us in our suffering and comforts and befriends us. He does this by the exercise of His gracious providence so that circumstances are ordered or friends are directed to us in such a way as to bring comfort and encouragement. We discover that Paul is not penning empty words when he writes "We know that all things work together for good to them that love God" (Ro. 8: 28). The God who "works all things after the counsel of His own will" (Ep. 1: 11) is "able to make all grace abound towards us" (2 Co. 9: 8). Jesus puts it as a logical argument: "If you then being evil know how to give good gifts unto your children, how much more shall your Father which is in heaven give good things to them that ask Him" (Mt. 7: 11). Luke's version of the saying focuses attention on the supreme gift: "How much more shall your heavenly Father give the Holy Spirit to them that ask Him?" (Lu. 11: 13).

To the Christian facing great pain, or reeling under some shattering disappointment, or wrestling with the lonely sorrow of bereavement, the reassurance of a heavenly Father's care comes as a healing

36

balm to a troubled soul. Henry Lyte's well-known hymn voices the response of the heart:

> Father-like He tends and spares us;
> Well our feeble frame He knows;
> In His hands He gently bears us,
> Rescues us from all our foes:
> Praise Him, praise Him
> Widely as His mercy flows.

CHAPTER 5

THE SYMPATHETIC CHRIST

It was a great sufferer who once cried out in agony, "Oh that I knew where I might find Him" (Jb. 23: 3). When we find ourselves groping in the darkness and feel numbed with pain, then God may seem to be so remote as to be unknowable. In fact this is what the Bible says about God, though of course it adds a vital qualification. So we are told that God dwells in light inaccessible. He is "the high and lofty One that inhabiteth eternity" (Is. 57: 15), but the prophet continues with the reassuring qualification, "I dwell in the high and holy place, with Him also that is of a contrite and humble spirit, to revive the spirit of the humble, and to revive the heart of the contrite ones." The apostle John, with the fulness of knowledge of one who had seen Isaiah's hopes realised in Jesus Christ, spoke the same message but with a glorious completeness, "No man has seen God at any time. The only begotten Son who is in the bosom of the Father He has declared Him" (Jn. 1: 18). That is why John describes Jesus as "the Word", for in Him God has made Himself known. That is why Jesus Himself summed it up so succinctly: "He that hath seen Me hath seen the Father" (Jn. 14: 9).

The good news of salvation begins here. To the sinner who has heard the threatening of God's law and has felt the sting of conviction in his own conscience, God seems to be hidden in the grim darkness of judgement. That is why it is like the dawn of a new day when he hears that the God of wrath is also the God of mercy and forgiveness, and that this mercy has been revealed in Jesus Christ. He does not need to speculate about what God may do with him or how God will react to him. He finds that God has stooped in grace and has clothed Himself with human nature and has taken the guilty sinner's place at Calvary. So Christ is the perfect revelation of the Father. In the words of Jesus he hears God speak. In the life of Jesus he sees God's righteousness lived out. In the death of Jesus he sees God's mercy reaching out to sinful men. In the resurrection of Jesus he sees the power which can make him a new creation. In the heavenly ministry of the ascended Christ he finds a mediator and an advocate through whom he can come boldly to God.

But this truth – that God is revealed uniquely in Christ – does not simply apply to the beginning of the Christian life, when the sinner finds himself freely forgiven and justified for Christ's sake. It continues to apply throughout his Christian life. Every time he comes to pray he takes his stand on the established basis of the finished work of Christ. Every time he approaches God's throne he comes through the one and only and all-sufficient mediator. That is why he comes with confidence and indeed with boldness.

But what makes this truth all the more wonderful is that the Christ in whom God made Himself known was the man Jesus. There was no make-believe about the incarnation. Mary truly did conceive a child in her womb, although instead of a human father there was the supernatural agency of the Holy Spirit. Mary did give birth to a baby who in due course became a boy and a man. Luke underlines His humanity when he sums up His childhood: "And Jesus increased in wisdom and stature, and in favour with God and man" (2: 52). He never ceased to be the Son of God, the second Person of the blessed Trinity. When He laid aside His glory to don our humanity He did not relinquish His Godhead. This is the great mystery of the incarnation which led Charles Wesley to pen his great hymn:

> "Veiled in flesh the godhead see,
> Hail the incarnate deity,
> Pleased as man with men to dwell,
> Jesus our Emmanuel."

Wesley in another hymn aptly spoke of the mystery of it.

> "Our God, contracted to a span,
> Incomprehensibly made man."

This essential humanity of the Son of God incarnate is strikingly emphasised in the epistle to the Hebrews. It is noticeable that the name which is especially applied to Him in this epistle is "Jesus". In the epistles generally He is more usually presented as "Jesus Christ" or "the Lord Jesus Christ". Now Jesus is the normal designation in the four gospels, which are of course describing His earthly life and ministry. So it is as if Hebrews keeps reminding us that this One, who has been exalted to the glorious position of authority at the Father's right hand, remains Jesus, the One who died at Calvary. This does not mean that Hebrews in any way moderates the New Testament witness to the deity of Christ. In fact the opening chapter is one of the most majestic statements in the whole of Scripture of the surpassing glory of the Son. It is therefore all the more striking and, as we shall see, all the more comforting, that the exalted Son is still our Jesus.

This leads to a very practical application in the realm of suffering. We have a sympathetic Saviour who fully understands our pains and so is able to meet us in our hours of need. Because He lived a full human life He does not view us from some detached position but rather from the stand-point of a fellow sufferer. "For we have not a high priest who cannot be touched with the feeling of our infirmities; but was in all points tempted like as we are, yet without sin" (He. 4: 15). "Though He were a Son, yet learned He obedience by the things which He suffered and being made perfect He became the author of eternal salvation unto all them that obey Him" (He. 5: 8-9).

This is applied to the Christian in his prayer life. Because our High Priest is so sympathetic we do not need to come hesitantly. On the contrary, "Let us therefore come boldly unto the throne of grace, that we may obtain mercy, and find grace to help in time of need" (He. 4: 16). It is also applied to the spiritual contest in which the Christian is involved in the arena of faith. As he runs the race set before him he must "lay aside every weight and the sin which doth so easily beset" him. Above all he must look away to Jesus. His incentive to do this is that Jesus is "the pioneer and perfecter of faith". He has run the race and faced all the obstacles in running. He has won the prize and from the end of the course He beckons and encourages the hard-pressed runners.

So in times of pain and suffering, when we scarce know where to turn, when even the warmest human sympathy fails to touch the deep-seated hurt, a hurt which is perhaps too deep for tears, we may remind ourselves that we have a heavenly sympathizer. He is no aloof deity reigning in remote splendour while we struggle on in the darkness. He has been this way Himself. He has drunk to the dregs the cup of pain. He has known an exquisite agony such as we shall never know. So we can sing with Michael Bruce:

"Though now ascended up on high,
He bends on earth a brother's eye;
Partaker of the human name
He knows the frailty of our frame.

Our fellow sufferer yet retains
A fellow-feeling of our pains;
And still remembers in the skies
His tears His agonies and cries.

In every pang that rends the heart
The Man of Sorrows had a part.
He sympathises with our grief
And to the sufferer sends relief."

But Scripture does not leave us with a vague general statement of the sufferings of Jesus. It does not simply record the main items of His suffering such as His sorrows, His pain, His death. It goes into detail and in moments of high revelation it draws the veil aside to let us see not only what He suffered, but how He suffered, not only His pains, but also His reactions. And all this is for our profit to help us, as Michael Bruce put it, "in the evil hour".

Those who have never known agonizing physical pain may be inclined to a superficial judgement in which they think pain is simply something to be borne with a stoic fortitude. But anyone who has known great pain will know how its persistence can have a wearing down effect. We are not like lodgers occupying a guest house where the condition of the house does not have too great a bearing on the residents. We are integrated personalities where our bodily condition is intimately linked with our thinking and our feeling. So continuing pain can lead to depression; it can produce an inability to think clearly; it can lead to a virtual paralysis of the will. Great pain is not of itself a great good, though it can be used by God to accomplish great good. It is a great evil, one of the grim consequences of our fallen humanity. Those who have spent sleepless

41

nights in physical agony or who have watched a loved one suffer will endorse all this. Others who have not known such pain at first hand may at least try to understand.

At such times it is good to reflect on the fact that the Scriptures say a great deal about the actual physical sufferings of Jesus. They were not of course the supreme pains, for the spiritual agony far surpassed them. But they were real and must neither be dismissed nor minimised. They are certainly not minimised in the prophetic Psalm which was on the Saviour's lips in His moment of supreme agony when He cried, "My God, my God, why hast Thou forsaken Me?" It is in that same Psalm 22 that we get some of the most vivid pictures of intense physical pain: "I am poured out like water, and all my bones are out of joint. . . . My strength is dried up like a potsherd; and my tongue cleaveth to my jaws . . . I may tell all my bones."

With that background and with the further presentation of the suffering servant of Jehovah in Isaiah 53 we turn to the gospel narrative. There the detailed picture of His pains is built up. He is brutally treated by the soldiers as they hit Him in the face and force a crown of thorns on His brow. He is scourged at Pilate's command, and scourging was such a severe punishment that men sometimes died under the brutal lashing. On His lacerated back He had to carry the rough wood of His cross. He was nailed to the tree and endured without the anaesthetic drug, which He refused, the cruel torture of crucifixion, as physical pain blended with a consuming thirst. How much is summed up in the brief but poignant statement of the Apostles' Creed: "He suffered under Pontius Pilate, was crucified, dead and buried."

But if in our physical pains we can look away to Jesus who for our sakes endured the cross, then too in our hours of mental distress we may find in Him the sympathetic High Priest who suffered the most intense assaults that a human mind has ever endured. The stress for Him was constant, as throughout His ministry He was looking forward to the cross. For us the future is mercifully veiled. Indeed people will say that if they had known what they were going to have to endure they could not have faced it. But for Jesus the future was not veiled. Immediately after His baptism He is tempted by Satan to take the easy path, but He refuses, for His face is set towards the hard and lonely path of pain and death. When Peter, after his moment of glory in confessing Jesus to be the Son of God, becomes the mouthpiece of Satan to suggest to Jesus that suffering and rejection and death are unthinkable, he is rebuked. In fact they are the way forward and the shadow of the coming agony is always with Him. This is the sympathetic High Priest who comes to us in our darkest hours when friends cannot calm the turmoil of our mind.

But there are further explicit mentions of the mental pains He endured, which are such an encouragement and strength to us. Listen to His appeal to His disciples for their sympathetic support: "My soul is exceeding sorrowful even unto death. Tarry ye here and watch with me." As man, Jesus went through a storm of mental darkness in which He cried out for human sympathy from His disciples. They failed, and their failure added to the pain and wrung from Him the remonstrance, "Could you not watch with Me one hour?" When human support fails us in our hour of supreme testing it is good to know that we have a High Priest who appreciates the inner rending which comes with intense loneliness of spirit.

His pain was not simply the reaction to their temporary failure. They forsook Him and fled; Peter denied Him; Judas betrayed Him. In days of pain and stress when the world is hostile and men either misunderstand us or misrepresent us, it is an enduring strength to have solid friends who stand by us through thick or thin. But to face betrayal when we need support, to find a trusted friend turning into a broken reed, this is to have misery compounded with the bitterness of disappointment. Yet in such a bleak moment of solitary grief we find a heavenly supporter who once walked this same path.

There was further mental stress He had to endure. He was by birth and upbringing a Jew. He was in fact the promised Messiah of Israel. He had grown up in a land suffering the oppression of Rome. He knew all about the bloody massacre of the Galileans by Pilate and the extortionate demands of the Roman exchequer. He knew too how Jews hated it all and longed for deliverance and freedom. Yet here is the great lover of Jerusalem being rejected by His own people and handed over by them to Gentiles to crucify. Could blind misunderstanding be more callous than this?

It is hard to suffer, but harder still to see others we love suffer. How much more intense the pain when their suffering is caused by our actions, even though those actions have been demanded so insistently by our conscience that there has been no alternative. To take a step which involves great personal sacrifice is costly, but the cost is even greater when others are involved. And Mary was involved. She who had borne the shame when He was conceived, now faced the final agony whose dark shadow had for so long stretched across her brightest hours. But if it was agony for Mary to see Him die as an object of public ridicule, how much more was it agony for Jesus to see her suffer. As He commends her to the care of John His words are not only an echo of His deep love for her, but of His deep pain that she must suffer.

When we turn to the central area of His sufferings when He, the Holy One, was made sin for us, we are obviously moving into a region which is not only beyond anything we could or will experience, but ultimately beyond our imagination. To hear Him cry in His moment of awful dereliction is to sense from afar a pain which beggars description. But if this moment far transcended all the physical and mental pains He endured, then how much more is His atoning death a pledge to us of His unending sympathy for us. Whatever pains we face, whatever the loneliness or the misunderstanding, whatever the grief of spirit, nothing will ever begin to compare with the darkness of Golgotha. So, because He drank so deeply of bitter suffering, He is able to steady our hand as we drink what for us is a bitter draught but is, by comparison with His, a diluted cup.

CHAPTER 6

THE HOLY GHOST THE COMFORTER

"I will pray the Father and He shall give you another Comforter." This was Jesus' promise to His disciples (Jn. 14: 16). The qualifying word "another" indicated that the Spirit who was to come would take the place of Jesus, and fulfil to the disciples the same ministry which Jesus had exercised during His years with them. He knew how they must feel at the prospect of His leaving them. He was the focus of their hopes, the source of their strength, the centre of their life. Yet He speaks to them of going away so that they will not see Him again. Then comes His reassurance: "I will not leave you orphans." They will not be bereft of a helper. They will not be forsaken. Another Comforter will come and He will be with them forever.

The Greek word translated "comforter" in the Authorised Version, is sometimes transliterated in hymns as "the Paraclete". In Greek usage the term "paracletos" means, literally, someone called alongside to help. It was used, for example, of an advocate in a law court who was summoned to your defence. So the heavenly paraclete is the strengthener, the counsellor, the supporter. He comes to us in our weakness to impart His strength. He comes in our perplexity to give His guidance. He comes in our turmoil to bestow His calm.

It was at first sight baffling to the disciples that Jesus should say, "It is expedient for you that I go away." They might have understood it if He had explained His proposed absence as an unfortunate necessity, but instead He speaks of it as being to their advantage. Clearly then it must mark an even greater progress in their knowledge of God. They must have asked themselves if anything could

45

ever compare with the amazing experience of walking the roads of Galilee in the personal company of God incarnate. How then could any new development be an advance on that? The answer was that when the Spirit came the companionship which they had enjoyed would be even richer and more intimate. The Son of God had come right alongside them. But the Spirit of God would take up His residence in their lives. They would be like the temple of the Old Testament – God's dwelling place.

If we are to grasp something of the working of the Holy Spirit in the life of the Christian, we need to listen to what the Scriptures have to say about who the Holy Spirit is. It is at this basic point that many Christians are rather vague. It is no wonder therefore that they live at times (or perhaps it would be better to say they try to live) as if there were no Holy Spirit. For too long and in too many cases the Spirit of God has been the forgotten or at least the neglected factor. But without Him there would be no Christian experience at all. Our knowledge of Him and our enjoyment of His indwelling presence will therefore have a major bearing on our growth in holiness, our joy in service and, in the context of the present book, our endurance in suffering and sorrow.

We need to be reminded at the outset that the Holy Spirit is divine in the same exalted sense that the Father is God and the Son is God. In the mysterious unity of the Godhead He is the third Person of the blessed Trinity. When a Christian is baptized the Spirit is invoked along with the Father and the Son. Similarly, when the benediction is pronounced the fellowship of the Holy Spirit is in the same bracket as the grace of the Son and the love of the Father. It is not surprising then that Peter in his conversation with Ananias can equate lying to the Holy Spirit with lying to God (Ac. 5: 3, 4, 9). Paul echoes the same truth when he declares that only the Holy Spirit knows the thoughts of God (1 Co. 2: 10).

Furthermore, we must emphasise what is so often misunderstood, that He is a person. It is easy to speak of the Spirit in terms of an influence. Just as we might speak of the spirit of a great national figure like Churchill continuing to make an impact after his death, so it is possible to conceive of the Spirit of God as simply the influence of God in the world and the impact of that influence on men. But this is a totally false notion. We are not dealing with some impersonal force, but with a person who is as identifiably and really a person as the Father and the Son. So in the Bible He speaks to men – and speech is essentially an activity of a person (Ac. 8: 29, 10: 19, 13: 2, 16: 6-7). He may be grieved (Ep. 4: 30) and obviously it is not possible to grieve or hurt an influence. So the Holy Spirit is revealed as the third person of the Trinity who plays His own distinctive part in the work of redemption.

There is no time to enlarge on the variety of His activities. But in passing it may be noted that He was present in the act of creation, bringing order, design and life (Ge. 1: 2, Ps. 33: 6, Jb. 26: 13, 33: 4). He has been active in the work of salvation, whether in the realm of revelation, giving us the Scriptures through His chosen men (2 Ti. 3: 13, 2 Pe. 1: 21) or in the realm of the incarnation. It was He who gave Mary power to conceive the Messiah (Lu. 1: 35), who anointed Jesus at His baptism (Lu. 3: 22), led Him to His temptation (Mt. 4: 1) and worked in Him in His teaching (Lu. 4: 18) and in His works (Mt. 12: 28). It was He who enabled the suffering Saviour to offer Himself without spot to God (He. 9: 14), who was present in the miracle of the resurrection (Ro. 1: 4) and present also in the Ascension (Jn. 16: 8, Ac. 2: 33).

He has not only acted in laying the foundation of salvation, He has continued to apply the fruits of Christ's saving work to the souls of men. He finds us dead in sin (Ep. 2: 1-3) ignorant of our condition and ignorant of God (1 Co. 2: 14), carnal and rebellious (Ro. 8: 7, Ep. 2: 13). He enlightens our minds (1 Co. 2: 10-14) and so convicts us of our sin (Jn. 16: 8), granting us the gifts both of repentance and of faith (Ac. 5: 31, 16: 14). Having led us to saving faith in Christ He gives us assurance that we have been accepted by God (Ro. 8: 15-16), satisfies the deep thirst of our soul (Jn. 7: 37-39) and in accomplishing the great miracle of the new birth (Jn. 3: 5-8) He makes us new people – a new creation.

There is another important truth which has a direct bearing on His work in our hearts. It is presented in the centuries old statement of the Nicene Creed: "He proceedeth from the Father and the Son." This truth is rooted in the New Testament revelation. Thus on the one hand the Spirit is given by the Father to the disciples at the request of the Son (Jn. 14: 16, 26 cf. Ga. 3: 14); on the other the Son is the one who graciously gives the Spirit and in this gift He Himself comes in person to His disciples (Jn. 7: 39, 15: 26, Ac. 2: 33). This means that the Holy Spirit makes both the Father and the Son real to us.

We have already seen that one great source of comfort in our suffering is the realisation that God Almighty is our Father. He cares for us. He loves us. He watches over us in our troubles. He pities us in our misery. But how do we grasp these truths, especially when our minds are numbed with grief or tense with anxiety? It is the Spirit who comes from the Father who pierces the dullness of our minds to light up with a blaze of meaning the glory of the fatherhood of God.

It is not enough, however, to have clear ideas about God, important though that certainly is. When we suffer, our hearts are sore. We may be able to reason about the situation logically, and may understand in some measure the truths of God which are the answer to our need. But often the inner cry of the soul is for the ability to translate these ideas in the mind into warm feelings in the heart. Here again it is the role of the Spirit to do precisely this. He not only enlightens our mind to grasp that God loves us, but He sheds the love of God abroad in our hearts (Ro. 5: 5) and we can say with a new depth of feeling, even in the midst of our pain and our tears, "I know my Father loves me!" It is because He works deeply within the soul that we can cry out in a prayer of childlike confidence, "Abba, Father".

He proceeds also from the Son. Our Saviour has been exalted to glory. He is at the right hand of God interceding for us. But He is not the remote heavenly Christ. He is the sympathetic Jesus who recalls His own pains and cries. Again we cry out from our heart to know and feel His sympathy. Yet it is not enough simply to reflect on the truth that we have a sympathetic high priest. We need to feel the touch of His hand upon us. It is then that the words of Jesus come home: "I will not leave you orphans, I will come to you". So the Holy Spirit is the one through whose agency the heavenly Christ dwells in our hearts. Christ does not flit through our minds. He takes up His residence in the heart and it is in the person of the Holy Spirit that He comes to us. It is as the Spirit works in the inner man that we know the length and breadth and depth and height of the love of Christ which passes knowledge (Ep. 3: 18-19).

In times of pain or sorrow prayer is a great comfort, but it can also be very difficult. We may be shattered by some devastating blow, or we may be worn down by a long-drawn-out misery. But in either case we may find it hard to pray. Indeed we may be in such a state of turmoil that we scarcely know what to pray for. Paul comments on this very situation as he speaks of the Spirit as the intercessor

within our hearts whose prayers are an echo of the heavenly intercessor at the right hand of the throne of God. The Saviour prays for
us; the Spirit prays for us; and we in our stammering uncertainty
can fling ourselves on the tender mercies of our God. "We know
not what to pray for as we ought" – we have sadly vindicated that
statement. But there is more to it than that. "The Spirit Himself
maketh intercession for us with groanings that cannot be uttered"
(Ro. 8:26).

Then, again, it is the Spirit's presence in our heart which gives us
assurance not only that our prayer is heard, but also that God is able
to do far beyond our asking. His ability, which we so often try to
confine within the constricting limits of our own weak faith, knows
no bounds. Even beyond what we think He is able to do, God is
capable of infinitely more. But we are not left to try and grope after
this overwhelming truth that all power belongs to God. He has
already given us a pledge. If we have experienced the power of the
Spirit in the miracle of our own new birth, if we have already felt
His strength in the battle against sin, here is the dynamic token that
God is able to do even greater things. The power of the Spirit,
which we have already proved, is the measure by which to assess
the resources of our God. Listen to Paul as he sums it all up in an
ascription of praise to the God who answers prayer: "Now unto
Him that is able to do exceeding abundantly above all that we ask
or think, according to the power that worketh in us, unto Him be
glory in the church by Christ Jesus throughout all ages, world
without end, Amen" (Ep. 3:20-21).

When we are being painfully tested, and are perhaps tempted to
feel either self-pity or resentment against God, we yet know deep
down that this is not the way. The way of submission to the will of
God is the way of ultimate peace of soul. But how can we submit
when every fibre of our being is crying out in protest against the
blows which seem to rain upon us. The answer is to be found in
Paul's enumeration of the various elements in the fruit of the Spirit
(Ga. 5:22 ff.). When the life of the Spirit of God is flowing in our
souls like the sap in the vine, then fruit will be borne. Where there
might be bitterness there will be love. Where there might be
unmitigated grief there will be joy. Where there might be turmoil
of soul there will be peace. Resentment against others gives way to
forbearance. Insensitivity to the pains of others gives way to gentleness. A selfish immersion in our own problems is countered by the

fruit of goodness. Prone as we are to falter in face of the hardness of the road and the magnitude of the problems, to us the Spirit imparts faith. In face of the ugly tendency to rebel against God there is the growth of meekness as we learn to submit. Where pain and sorrow would lead men and women to lash out in bitterness at their miseries, the Spirit teaches self-control. The fruit of the Spirit is not some theoretical outcome of an inner spiritual experience, it is the actual outworking in our daily life, and in our sorrows, of the gracious and fruitful operation of the Spirit in our hearts.

In face of the pains of a suffering world the Christian should long to be of service. He wants to sympathise and to minister to others. But where will he find resources for this? The reply to this question is the reflection that among the various gifts which the Spirit imparts to His people, the supreme one which He grants to those who seek with all their hearts, is love. This means not only the enjoyment of God's love in our hearts, but the ability to reflect that love in our care for others.

This is true not only of the individual Christian, it is also true of the Church. The congregation of God's people is intended to be a caring community. How often someone broken by pain or stricken by personal grief has found healing of mind in a warm and caring church fellowship. But tragically, and in stark contrast, there have been situations where the loneliness of grief or the weight of the burden has been accentuated by a coldness and apparent indifference on the part of the church.

The conclusion one can draw from all this is that the Christian needs to take very seriously the firm command of Paul – and notice that it is not a plea or an exhortation but a plain command – "Be filled with the Spirit". He draws the contrast with being filled with wine. When a man is drunk he is no longer himself; he is less of a man than he might be. But by contrast, when a man is filled with the Spirit and mastered by the Spirit, he is more of a man than he could be by any means he might devise. In the same way, when a number of such Spirit-filled Christians are knit together in the fellowship of a local church, God has an instrument of mercy in His hands to help many a stumbling soul to regain his footing in the way that leads to life.

Much of the New Testament teaching on the work of the Spirit is summed up in two illustrations used by the apostle Paul in writing to the Ephesians (1: 13-14). The Spirit is God's seal. Now a seal stamps the image of its user on a document and, in giving the Spirit, God re-makes the sinner in His own image: the likeness which Adam forfeited by his sin. But a seal is also an authenticating mark. It declares that the document is valid and will be honoured. So too the Spirit is God's assuring word in the heart that the promises of adoption and blessing are truly ours. It is the sealing of the Spirit which gives us the ultimate assurance of our salvation, and gives us confidence to come in prayer to our heavenly Father. We may be tempted in the darkness to doubt God's care, but the Spirit confirms God's ownership so that we can say, "I am His and He is mine!"

The other word Paul uses is translated in the A.V. "earnest" and in the R.S.V. "guarantee". It is a word drawn from the commercial field. The earnest was the down payment made by the purchaser. It not only meant that he established a claim to the goods, but also that he committed himself to complete the transaction. So God in giving the Spirit has established His authority over us, but He has also committed Himself, by this generous first instalment, to complete what He has begun. Redemption means total deliverance. Already through the Spirit we have been brought to the Redeemer. We have found cleansing in His blood, and new life in communion with God. But there are greater things ahead. There is the final deliverance from sin and from the frailty of our mortal condition. There is the glory of heaven when not only sin will be banished, but all its sorry entail of sickness and pain, sorrow and tears. When the darkness sets in and the road is uphill the Spirit who is within us whispers, "Look up and lift up your heads for your redemption draweth nigh" (Lu. 21 : 28).

In one of His forceful parables Jesus told of a man who had an unexpected guest at midnight. Not having enough food he went to knock up a neighbour who, not surprisingly, was unwilling to be disturbed. But his reluctance had to give way to the insistence of the man at the door who refused to take "No" for an answer. It was certainly not Jesus' intention to misrepresent God as a reluctant deity whose hand has to be forced. On the contrary, God's liberality overflows. But what He had in mind were the quality and the earnestness of our praying. It is not the perfunctory utterance of a few petitions which constitutes prayer. It is the desperate entreaty which will not be refused. So, says Jesus, "Ask and it shall be given you; seek, and ye shall find; knock, and it shall be opened unto you." But what are we looking for? What do we receive? Matthew's version (Mt. 7: 11) speaks of God giving us good things, all those blessings which are needful for us in every test and trial of life. Luke however speaks of the supreme gift from which all the others derive (Lu. 11: 5-13). It is the gift we have had in view throughout this chapter. "If ye then, being evil, know how to give good gifts unto your children: how much more shall your heavenly Father give the Holy Spirit to them that ask Him?"

CHAPTER 7

FINDING A PURPOSE IN PAIN

Modern man lives in a very small world. At the very same time, when his horizons seem to be expanding as space is probed and the frontiers of research in many fields are pushed further and further, he finds himself increasingly shut in by a universe which yields him no spark of meaning. There is no God, so he claims, nor is there anything beyond the grave. His ultimate frontiers are the present state of human knowledge and his own obituary. There is nothing beyond, apart from further scientific advance, and even that is curtailed by the fact that it is within a universe where the absence of any spiritual reality means an absence of any ultimate meaning. The barren landscape of the moon may excite the imagination, but it gives no answer to the deepest questions of life. The data furnished by the radio telescope may further the astonomer's knowledge of the universe, but they do not tell him anything about the issues of life and death, of pain and sorrow.

To live in such a godless world is to live in hopelessness and to die in despair. Suffering is utterly pointless and the best one can do is to find some means of alleviating the distress. But the Christian is persuaded that this world is not that kind of blind alley. The present physical universe is not the extraordinary outcome of some fortuitous convergence of material forces. History is not some turbulent stream of events tumbling over the rocks and finally losing itself in the sands of meaninglessness. The world bears the stamp firmly laid on it of a purposeful Creator. History bears clear evidence, not of the inter-play of blind economic forces or of mere material factors, but of the providential direction of a personal God.

The world about us bears the marks of the curse of God, but it also gives clear evidence of the grace of God. History exhibits all the cruelties and vices of sinful men, but it is also vibrant with the redemptive purposes of God. So pain is not some accidental excrescence on life to which one can only react with a shrug of despairing acquiescence. Even in pain there is meaning to be found, and the Christian aims, not merely to survive the buffetings which suffering brings, but to learn the lessons which God is teaching him. His faith is not a prescription for survival, but is the divinely-given key to unlock some at least of the mysteries of the pains and griefs which inevitably beset him.

To put this in personal terms and at an individual level, the Christian faces his own suffering with challenging questions. He does not ask merely, "How can I find strength to face this test?" This question he certainly does ask, and the answer he discovers in the grace of God. But it is not his final question. The ultimate query is, "What is God teaching me through this time of suffering?" Allied to that is the further practical consideration, "How am I to apply the lessons I learn to my own profit, to help others, and above all to glorify God?"

One of the most obvious values, in what might otherwise seem to be pointless pain, is that it impels us to seek God in a far more earnest way. Read the Psalms and listen to the cry of pain and at times of sheer anguish. What is the recurring response? It is to seek God with desperate earnestness. "As the hart panteth after the water brooks so panteth my soul after thee O God." Likewise, it was when Paul was struggling with his "thorn in the flesh" that he was driven to plead with God for deliverance, and then to discover a greater blessing in the promise: "My grace is sufficient for thee."

The child may run in the sunlight and scarcely be aware of his parents walking behind him, but in a pitch dark night on a country road he clutches his father's hand very tightly. So the Christian discovers that there is great danger of self-reliance and forgetfulness of God when the skies are blue and the circumstances are favourable. But when the clouds gather and the going is rough he finds himself compelled to turn with a new urgency to his heavenly Father. Indeed he can later praise God that the trouble came because it drove him into his Father's arms.

As pain drives us to seek the Lord so it can be a means of disclosing more of God's character to us. We may have correct doctrinal notions about the meaning of "grace" but the word throbs with new life when we have felt the gracious hand of God laid on us in our sickness. We may have acknowledged the omnipotence of God in theory, but it is in our weakness that His strength is made perfect, and in our despair that His power is discovered to be all-sufficient. We may have had vague ideas of God's fatherhood, but when we have seen Him by faith in the valley of tears or of disappointment, then we know, not only in the mind, but in the heart, that "like as a father pitieth his children so the Lord pitieth them that fear Him, for He knoweth our frame, He remembereth that we are dust" (Ps. 103: 13). The chastening may have been sore and indeed so severe that at times we felt we could not endure much more, but then we found that it was a study course to teach us His love. "Whom the Lord loveth He chasteneth and scourgeth every son whom He receiveth" (He. 12: 6). So pain is transformed from being a bitterly resented intrusion, into an avenue to more intimate communion with God.

To glorify God in our sufferings implies an audience which is moved, by the evidence of God's grace in the sufferer, to glorify the Lord. This audience does not comprise only men and women. Indeed, because some of the triumphs of grace are won in the intimacy of the sufferer's own room, or indeed of his own soul, there may be no human onlooker at all. None the less, there are always witnesses, for in Scripture the believer is surrounded by an invisible host of angelic powers. There are not only those who are hostile, and against whom we "wrestle", but there are those who are "ministering spirits sent forth to minister to those who shall be heirs of salvation" (He. 1: 14). They are pictured in 1 Corinthians 11: 10 as being the unseen watchers when the church gathers for worship. In Ephesians 3: 9 they view the church as God's object lesson in which they see mirrored "the manifold wisdom of God". In the book of the Revelation the host of heaven joins with the redeemed in worship. They have not known sin but they hear the song of those who have come through great tribulation and from whom flows the great refrain, "Unto Him that loved us and loosed us from our sins in His own blood and hath made us kings and priests unto God and His Father, to Him be glory and dominion for ever and ever" (Rev. 1: 5-6). So the angelic worship in heaven continues to be the adoring wonder of those who marvel at what God has done with poor sinful mortals.

To the sick person struggling with the lonely darkness of a

sleepless night, or to the bereaved in the bleak emptiness of loss, it is a strength to see their pain in the wide context of the purposes of God. God will be glorified in all things. The angels who sang together at the dawn of the world's creation, and at the dawn of the new creation at Bethlehem, who rejoice over every sinner that repents, also praise God as they see the patience and the meekness, the fortitude and the deepening faith of the suffering Christian. So my pains and my sorrows may be a crushing burden, but I find them lighter when I discover that in and through them God is displaying His grace, not only to me, but to the hidden onlookers of the sky.

Then, again, the Christian's reaction to suffering can be a powerful reinforcement to the gospel. The world today faces a babel of conflicting voices and of competing ideologies. A natural human response is to ask of any political or religious message, "Does it work?" A mere theory, no matter how persuasively it is presented, is of no interest to the ordinary man as he struggles with the pressures of living – and ultimately of dying. What he asks for is solid evidence for the claims being made. How compelling therefore is the testimony of a very ordinary Christian who in the midst of great suffering has not lapsed into self-pity or bitterness, but has demonstrated a deep peace of soul, and indeed a remarkable joy in the face of trial! Here is a living vindication of the gospel. Here is an authentication in flesh and blood of the message that Jesus Christ is mighty to save. The preacher, whose call to the unconverted is backed by the evidence of victory in adversity, has a more powerful support for his message than any number of cogent arguments which he is able to muster.

The lessons we learn in our sufferings are not only profitable to us personally, but they fit us to help others. So Paul writes to the Corinthians of the comfort of God and of the further aim in view, "that we may be able to comfort them which are in any trouble, by the comfort wherewith we ourselves are comforted of God" (2 Co. 1 : 4). To comfort others we need to learn to be sensitive to their deepest needs. A superficial word of passing sympathy only mocks by its sheer formality. What is required is the sympathy which comes right alongside and feels and grieves with the sufferer. But much sensitivity may itself be learnt through much pain, for it is true that some of the great sympathisers have been – and perhaps still are – great sufferers.

To help others requires also gentleness. The brusque approach or the hearty dismissal of the problem only adds to the pain. When a man's body is racked with pain he needs the nursing skill of one whose firm hands have also a gentle touch. And when someone is torn by sorrow or beset by the depression which accompanies suffering, he needs a gentle approach and a loving care. To have faced great physical pain oneself is to appreciate what rough handling can mean and to induce a gentle concern; similarly, to have suffered deeply is to learn lessons which will be applied in a gracious ministry to others.

But as well as sensitivity and gentleness, the experience of God's peace in our pains can lend us an authority in our ministry. It will not be an authority to which we will make explicit reference, but if the background of our attempts to help others is the lessons learnt in our own pains and sorrows, then there will inevitably be a compelling note in what we have to say. We are not reciting our set piece like the doorstep visitors from one of the cults, who have been well drilled in presenting their case. Nor are we simply quoting the appropriate texts of Scripture, vitally important though those texts certainly are. We are rather echoing what we ourselves have learnt from those texts and above all from the God who in our dark hours made them a word of blessing to our own souls. Indeed there are times when it is the sufferer who seems most in need of help who becomes the greatest help to others and those who went to comfort or sympathise are themselves helped and blessed by the overwhelming evidence of the grace of God.

Sick beds have often become great places of intercession and many of the greatest exponents of prayer have been among those who, to outward appearances, were hopelessly restricted. To be cut down in one's prime by an illness or an accident is to face the frustration of a life of inactivity and of seeming uselessness. Yet for many such a condition has become a wide open door to avenues of fruitful ministry which could never have been exercised amid the pressures of a busy life. When Amy Carmichael of Dohnavour was permanently invalided, it seemed unmitigated tragedy. But her bed was to become her pulpit, her counselling centre and above all her prayer base from which blessing flowed out, not only to South India, but also across the world. As I was writing this chapter I broke off to visit an old lady in her eighties. Her life constricted within the limits of an old people's home and her sight fast failing, she could easily become tearful and depressed. It was, however, like light in the darkness to be reminded that in prayer she was still wielding a ministry which reached far beyond the confines of her little room and touched with blessing men and women to the far ends of the earth.

"Whoso offereth praise glorifieth me" (Ps. 50: 23). If then our chief aim in life and in death is to glorify God, praise and thanksgiving must play a prominent part. But praise wells up with a new freshness when it is prompted by an awareness of God's goodness and mercy. The Psalmist bursts into praise: "I will bless the Lord at all times, his praise shall continually be in my mouth" (Ps. 34: 1). He is not however content with a solitary act of worship, and so he summons others to join him, "O magnify the Lord with me and let us exalt His name together". It is because of what God has done for him that he is overflowing with thanksgiving. "I sought the Lord and He heard me and delivered me from all my fears." To see only the darkness of sorrow, or to feel only the presence of pain, is to know a deepening bitterness of spirit. But to trace the evidence of God's providence in it all and to discover each new day that "His compassions fail not, they are new every morning. Great is Thy faithfulness" (Lam. 3: 22-23), these are stepping stones to higher ground where with full hearts we praise and magnify the Lord who is able to make all grace abound.

Peter has a further lesson in view as he reflects on suffering as God's furnace in which He tests the quality of our faith (1 Pe. 1: 7). Like the goldsmith who uses the refining fire to purge out the dross and to expose the pure gold, God destroys a spurious profession by means of suffering, but by that very same instrument He exhibits the abiding worth of a genuine faith which, says Peter, is much more genuine than even the purest gold which shall one day perish. But God not only tests the reality of faith, He also deepens and strengthens it through suffering. His aim indeed is that our faith shall be so refined that at the coming of Christ it will receive its due acclaim. Since, however, we shall then cast all our crowns before Him, the "praise and honour and glory" which the Lord shall ascribe to our triumphant faith will simply be the reflection of His own glory. This is the prospect which, for Peter, makes the most bitter trial joyful. God is perfecting the Christian's faith. God will complete the process and will finally exhibit that faith, which the world has so greatly despised, in all its essential worth.

Another purpose which suffering serves to fulfil is to detach us from this world and to "set our affections on things above and not on things on the earth" (Col. 3 : 2). When John urges us, "Love not the world", he does not refer to the created order, in which we see so much evidence of the Creator's power and wisdom that we are led to praise and worship. He refers rather to the world as an organised human structure in which God is rejected, His laws flouted and His gospel ignored. It is this world which is one of the great foes of the church and of the believer. The world however, does not always appear in its naked hostility. The devil is too much a master of strategy to utilise the resources of the world along one line only. So there are times when the world is presented in a very plausible way. Its material comforts, its popular esteem, its satisfying pleasures, its agencies for realising personal ambitions – these and many other factors are used to wean the Christian's affections from God. Imperceptibly the pilgrim finds himself settling down in Vanity Fair, and before he realises what is happening, his standards are being adjusted downwards, and his appetite for spiritual things is being dulled.

It is often true that at such times only pain or loss will awaken us to the folly of living for things which are purely temporary. "The things which are seen are temporal, but the things which are not seen are eternal" (2 Co. 4: 18). The things which are seen have an incredibly potent influence upon us, until they are shown up, in the context of suffering, to be so much passing show. I remember talking to a woman who had been diagnosed as having cancer. She recalled, with her own amused irony, how they had been having a discussion on the proposed pattern for the lounge wallpaper in which doubtless there were differences of family opinion. How irrelevant it all now seemed in face of the sombre reality she had to confront. And how irrelevant so many of the apparently major concerns of life turn out to be in the face of sickness and death. To the man of the world suffering is a disastrous interruption of his enjoyment of the only world he either knows or desires. To the Christian it can be a sudden shock to arouse him from his worldliness and to point him afresh to higher concerns. Indeed to the man of the world pain can be fruitful, for it may prove to be the thin edge of the wedge of the gospel which prises open his deadened soul to receive the Word of life.

But if God aims by suffering to detach us from this world it is because He has a greater goal in view for us. Slum clearance is not an end in itself simply to satisfy the town planners, its ultimate aim is to move people to better homes. So in all God's dealings, which at times may appear harsh, He is gently and graciously preparing us for removal. To change the analogy, like a gardener loosening the soil around the roots before transplanting, so the Lord breaks up the soil of our comfortable living and our persistent materialism. The fork which the heavenly gardener uses is a painful one but the ultimate aim is a new flowering in paradise.

CHAPTER 8

BIBLICAL CASE HISTORY (2)

PAUL

Such was his towering eminence in the early days of Christianity and such his massive contribution to the cause of the gospel, that it is all too easy to see Paul only as the spiritual giant, and to lose sight of his warm humanity. This is seen in the affection he inspired in others, so that the news that he would not see them again reduced the Christians at Caesarea to tears. It is reflected also in his own warm-hearted relationships, in which he not only contributed much to his friends but also received much from them. It is seen again in his hours of weakness when we catch glimpses of a lonely figure fighting great battles not only against his enemies outside but also within his own soul.

Not to appreciate how essentially human he was, is to fail to understand how intensely he suffered throughout his ministry. Apart from the Lord of glory, whose sufferings completely eclipse the pains of any of His servants, Paul appears as one of the great sufferers of Christian history. He stands in the same honourable tradition as the men and women of faith in the Old Testament whose endurance is recalled in Hebrews 11, for the faith by which he stood was the same faith which had enabled them to persist to the end.

His sufferings are mentioned explicitly in the Acts of the Apostles and also in his own letters, but in addition to this there are frequent passing references and brief allusions which fill out the picture. It does not require too much reading between the lines of his epistles to discover the constant battering which he took during his years of missionary endeavour. That is why he can administer such stinging rebukes to the spiritually lazy and complacent, for he himself was far removed from such attitudes. That is also why his words have comforted so many sufferers down the years, for they come from one who from his own bitter experience could write with an authority born of his own pain.

Physical pain he certainly knew. If, as seems most likely, his "thorn in the flesh" was some physical ailment, then clearly it was a chronic condition with which he had to learn to live. But there were also the constant privations involved in his hazardous journeys, with the recurring pattern of mob violence and beatings at the hands of unjust officials. His most graphic account comes in 2 Corinthians 11: 23-27. Here is a grim catalogue of savage beatings at the hands of both Jews and Gentiles; stoning by the mob at Lystra when he nearly died; dangerous journeys, facing not only the perils of robbers but the bitter enmity of those who hated his gospel; shipwreck on three occasions and the frequent physical misery of hunger, thirst and nakedness. It is no wonder he could silence his critics in Galatia: "From henceforth let no man trouble me: for I bear in my body the marks of the Lord Jesus" (Ga. 6: 17).

But he also knew the inner sufferings of mental struggle and of emotional pain. He knew fear in Corinth (witness the reassurance of which God saw him to stand in need in Acts 18: 9). He felt keenly the repeated humiliations which must have been all the more galling in view of his proud Rabbinic background and his own outstanding gifts. It must have been hard to endure the mockery of the Athenian intellectuals. Indeed it was such a bitter experience when he was ignominiously smuggled out of Damascus in a laundry basket that he records it as the climax of his sufferings (2 Co. 11: 32-33). Then there was the misunderstanding by fellow Christians which hurt him so deeply. There was the misrepresentation by Jews who treated him as a traitor to his nation, and, what was even worse, by some of his own converts who cut him to the quick by imputing false motives. One can feel the deep hurt of spirit as he protests to the Corinthians about the slanders they had tolerated; that he was out to further his own ends. The same hurt appears in his question to the Galatians, among whom he was also being mis-represented: "Am I, therefore become your enemy, because I tell you the truth?" (Ga. 4: 16).

To Paul "the care of all the churches" was a heavy burden, and any minister or elder involved in pastoral oversight will know, even if in a smaller context, something of this burden. For him it meant "to rejoice with them that do rejoice" and "to weep with them that weep". To share the griefs of Christians under persecution; to feel the deep sorrow of seeing some who promised well falling away; to see a developing work rent asunder by factional strife; these and many allied problems weighed heavily upon him. It is no wonder that in writing to the Colossians of his prayer for them he used a word which could be best translated by our English word "agony" – prayer for the churches was like a contest in an arena. So, again, he speaks of the desperate spiritual conflict with the powers of hell: "We wrestle not against flesh and blood, but against principalities, against powers, against the rulers of the darkness of this world; against spiritual wickedness in the heavenlies" (Ep. 6: 12).

There was also the crushing frustration of wanting to press on with the tasks to which God had called him, only to find himself held back by circumstances beyond his control. One notable example of such a frustrating experience was his imprisonment in Caesarea. It was not even that Felix the governor was keeping him in prison because of the gospel. It was at a more sordid level, for the corrupt governor was holding on in the hope of getting a bribe. Any missionary who has waited long for a visa, or known the seemingly interminable delay due to a corrupt or perhaps simply an inefficient bureaucracy, will know something of the frustration he must have faced.

The many burdens he carried must have seemed even heavier in the various times of loneliness he had to endure. He was obviously a man who greatly relished the company of his friends. To be alone was a sore trial. The desertion by Demas during his last imprisonment in Rome was clearly a sad blow. One can sense the cry of his heart for companionship as he urges Timothy again and again, "Do your best to come to me soon" (2 Ti. 4: 9), and also as he asks him to get Mark and bring him with him. Those who have tasted the loneliness of a pioneer work, whether at home or abroad; those who have faced the solitary grief of bereavement, or have been betrayed by someone they loved, will know how in such lonely hours the problems are magnified and the future becomes increasingly bleak.

But the real message for us is not so much in Paul's sufferings, as in his reaction to them; or perhaps it would be better to say in the lessons which God taught him through them. He proved to be a teachable pupil, although at times the instruction cost him dearly. It was a far cry from the self-righteous and self-confident Pharisee, who was so sure of the rightness of his own religious position, to the humble, suffering disciple in the school of Christ, ready to learn, even if learning meant great pain. Yet it is only in that school of suffering that the disciple will learn the deepest lessons.

Paul recognized the great dangers of spiritual pride – a peril which we are liable to ignore. He had been deeply humbled at the very outset of his Christian life by his experience on the Damascus road. But he realised that pride was always ready to raise its ugly head. So, although his "thorn in the flesh" caused him much pain, he came to see that there was a purpose behind it. It was God's way of checking his pride. He was quite specific on this point. God had given him such remarkable revelations that he was in danger of becoming spiritually elated to such a degree that he would slip into a conceited attitude. So his anguished questioning found its answer in the realisation that his suffering was God's instrument to keep him humble and so to remind him of his continuing dependence on the grace of God. Having learned this lesson he could praise God for the pain: "Most gladly therefore will I rather glory in my infirmities that the power of Christ may rest upon me" (2 Co. 12:9).

He had learnt well the role of praise in the Christian life. He knew how thanksgiving to God for all His mercies lifts the heart in times of discouragement and depression. But thanksgiving was not to him simply a means to an end, a convenient attitude to adopt in order to counteract feelings of distress or gloom. It emerged rather as he reflected on God's mercy to him. He could never forget the amazing grace which had reached him, blasphemer and persecutor that he was, and had made him a new creature. So while it was a cause for deep praise that "Christ Jesus came into the world to save sinners", it was a matter for overwhelming gratitude that he could qualify the word sinners by his own admission: "Of whom I am chief. But I obtained mercy." It was the mercy of God which was often in his mind, and which evoked such a constant response of praise. But he then learned that such praise and thanksgiving were fruitful in comforting and strengthening him. He discovered that, in stirring up our souls to bless the Lord, the primary aim of glorifying our God leads directly to our own personal blessing. To set our hearts on praising God is to have our hearts lifted above the problems and fears and anxieties which so trouble us.

Then, again, Paul learnt how to find strength in the word of the Lord. When he battled with his thorn in the flesh, it was the word of the Lord, "My grace is sufficient for thee", which brought peace of heart. When he faced the hostility of men, his reassurance

64

was in the Lord's promise: "I am with thee". His early training had steeped his mind in the Old Testament and its truths were there to be recalled in time of need. He spoke from his own experience when he reminded not only the church in Rome, but every Christian: "Whatsoever things were written aforetime were written for our learning that we through patience and comfort of the Scripture might have hope" (Ro. 15: 4).

At the same time he was intensely practical. He did not view faith as a substitute for action when the latter was within his powers. So he not only trusted his life into the Lord's hands, he also saw to it that when his nephew reported the assassination plot to him, the lad was quickly despatched to inform the Tribune, so that military protection could be provided. So, too, on board ship, he not only encouraged the others in the midst of the storm by sharing with them the message God had given him, but he also urged them to take food to be ready for the ordeal ahead; and when the sailors were preparing to abandon the ship he got the soldiers to cut away the boat. Paul is a constant reminder that the truly spiritual man is one who has his feet firmly on the earth of actual living and who uses the common wisdom God has given him as he tries to face his problems.

He reminds us also of the tensions involved in Christian living. Not for him some theory of entire sanctification with a sinless anticipation now of a future glory! He confessed that he had not yet attained, that he was not yet perfect. He pressed on towards the mark but was aware of the battle not only with the devil and the world without, but with the flesh within. He knew the overwhelming joy of the Lord in his heart, and at the very same time he felt deep and unceasing pain at the rejection by Israel of the Messiah. Life for him was a whole series of contrasts. On the one side there were the "afflictions, hardships, calamities, beatings, imprisonments, tumults, watchings, hunger"; but on the other side there were the graces wrought by the Holy Spirit in the life by means of these sufferings. So there were "purity, knowledge, forbearance, kindness, genuine love and truthful speech". There was human weakness, but also the power of God. There was an unceasing battle, but "the weapons of righteousness for the right hand and for the left". There was honour and also dishonour, ill repute and good repute. Life indeed was in a sense a constant dying, as he mortified the deeds of the body and as he worked out the crucifixion of the flesh and of the world; and yet in that very dying he found renewed life. In short his life was one of being "sorrowful yet always rejoicing, as poor yet making many rich; as having nothing and yet possessing everything" (2 Co. 6: 4-10).

He also discovered the value of Christian friends. Not for him the solitary approach to his difficulties. He was too aware of the truth which he himself expounded so powerfully, that a Christian is a member of the body of Christ, in which he not only draws his life from the head, but learns also the mutual dependence of the limbs on each other. So he wrote to the believers in Rome with warm personal greetings and with a keen anticipation of meeting them and of blessing not only imparted to them but received by him from them. When, at the end of the voyage, he reached Italy, with a court appearance before Caesar awaiting him, he was heartened by the friends who met him at Appii Forum and The Three Taverns. When he saw them, writes Luke, "he thanked God, and took courage" (Ac. 28: 15). His attitude is a reminder that we neglect fellowship with other Christians at our peril. The path to heaven is not a solitary road, but one where we join hands with others who are like us, pilgrims in the way to the celestial city.

All the time he had his heart fixed on that goal. He confessed to the Philippians that he had a desire "to depart and to be with Christ which was far better". Nevertheless, it was more expedient that he remain until the Lord summoned him, for there was work still to be done. He must press on with the tasks, but it would be with a forward look of expectancy. Beyond the battle was the victory, beyond the valley of humiliation the sunny uplands of heaven, beyond the contempt of men the crown of righteousness. Above all, to be "absent from the body" was to be "present with the Lord". So suffering and loss, however and whenever they might come, are set in the balance and found lacking when compared with the glory to be revealed. Worn and spent by his privations and the mental anguish of his ministry, he still remained buoyant. So he wrote, "We are troubled on every side, yet not distressed; we are perplexed, but not in despair; persecuted, but not forsaken; cast down, but not destroyed" (2 Co. 4: 8-9). Whence did he derive this steady joyfulness in the face of great suffering? It was from his confident assurance of the coming glory. "Knowing that he which raised up the Lord Jesus shall raise up us also by Jesus, and shall present us with you. . . . For which cause we faint not; but though

66

our outward man perish, yet the inward man is renewed day by day" (2 Co. 4: 14, 16).

In his letter to the Philippians he himself summed up the lessons learned: "I have learned in whatsoever state I am therewith to be content" (Ph. 4: 11). A lesson does not come automatically. It is not simply an experience which fits neatly into a slot with little attention paid to the process. It must be learned, and if the subject is an advanced one it may take much disciplined study and hard work. It will involve errors of judgement, and at times lines of research which prove to be a blind alley. But from the hard discipline of patient study, and from the knowledge gained from mistakes, the frontiers of knowledge and experience are pushed outwards. So, Paul, in the discipline of living, in the trials and afflictions and pains he had endured, had learned a great lesson. It was to see circumstances and events, both pleasant and unpleasant, enjoyable and painful, as being always subject to the sovereign God who moulds the pattern, not only for His own glory, but also for the benefit of His people. In submission to that sovereign direction, and in quiet reliance upon that gracious providence. Paul learnt that contentment of soul which enabled him to face every trial and to rejoice in the God who causes all things to work together for good to those who love Him.

PART III

Particular Applications

His purposes will ripen fast,
  Unfolding every hour;
The bud may have a bitter taste,
  But sweet will be the flower.

Blind unbelief is sure to err,
  And scan His work in vain;
God is His own interpreter,
  And He will make it plain.

W. Cowper

CHAPTER 9

BEREAVEMENT

The death of someone we love very deeply is one of the most over-whelming griefs in this life. Yet it is one that comes to most of us, apart from that minority whose plight is even more tragic in that they have neither relative nor friend whose passing they might mourn. To the ordinary individual, and to a shattered family unit, bereavement is the supremely crushing blow which makes so many other trials seem minor by comparison.

The loss may be sudden, when grief is compounded with shock and the bitterness of a parting without a chance to say good-bye. It may be the long anticipated end after a prolonged illness which stretched out the pain as the inevitable moment slowly approached. But however it comes, death is always a cruel blow because it tears lives apart and leaves behind the ragged edges of sundered relation-ships. Love, which has long delighted to embrace, finds itself clutching in agony at a void whose emptiness is darkened by the awful realisation that it will not be filled.

There is a recurring pain in bereavement. After the initial wave of sympathy, friends have to return to their normal pattern of home and work. But the lonely mourner cannot forget and easily resume the interrupted flow of life. Time may bring some measure of healing, but it also brings the anniversaries and the holidays which can be like stones on a beach, which for a time has been sandy, and then, suddenly and painfully for tender feet, reverts to its earlier jagged condition.

For the man with the restricted frontiers of a world without God there is nothing but despair, or the alleviation of the various escape mechanisms which help to dull the pain for a time. But for the

Christian there is an answer. Indeed one might say there are many answers, for the truths already considered in this book are particularly applicable at such a time. To know a Father's care, to feel the sympathy of Christ, to see a purpose in one's sorrow – all these are a solace in the grief. But the ultimate answer is the hope of heaven as the final reply to death.

But the hope of life beyond the grave, and of meeting with God in the uninterrupted bliss of heaven is not only a comfort in time of bereavement, it is the final answer also in all our sufferings. To reduce man to a creature bounded by this life is to turn life into one long mockery, for even its joys and achievements are but a passing show. But see him in the wide context of eternity and hope begins to blossom in the desert of despair. It is because of the solid confidence which the apostle Paul had in the final triumph that he saw the glory of the resurrection casting a light across the whole of life: "Therefore, my beloved brethren, be steadfast, immovable, always abounding in the work of the Lord, forasmuch as ye know that your labour is not in vain in the Lord" (1 Co. 15: 58).

The Christian will of course face the critical rejection of his hope by those who charge him with wishful thinking. None of us wants to die and the natural response to the inevitability of death is to hope against hope that there may be something beyond. But that is no more than a piece of rather desperate wishful thinking with no evidence to support it beyond our own wistfulness. So the argument runs – and indeed, there may be times of darkness when the Christian is tempted to ask himself, if, in fact, he is simply deluding himself by hoping for what may only be a figment of his imagination. Perhaps death is the end and there is nothing beyond but the chill void of non-existence. At that point he returns to the solid rock on which his hopes really rest, the resurrection of Jesus Christ. The ground for his confidence is not the projection of his own inner longings for survival beyond the grave both for himself and his loved ones, it is rather the solid reality of the great fact of all history, that the Christ who died and whose body lay in the tomb truly rose again from the dead.

When Paul expounds, in 1 Corinthians 15, the great hope of the resurrection of the body and the life everlasting, he roots it all in the resurrection of Christ. Indeed, he points out the logic of the denial of the resurrection of Christ: there would be no gospel of forgiveness, no hope for the future and we Christians, with all our confident

72

preaching, would be no more than objects of pity. But in fact, Paul triumphantly affirms, Christ did rise from the dead and became the first-fruits of them that slept.

The resurrection of Christ was not for Paul what it has become for some modern theologians, an attempt to express in first century myths the deep experience which the disciples had had of the impact of Jesus upon them. This impact, it is claimed, was so profound that they could not believe that His death was the end of it all. The myth of the godlike one who dies and rises was at hand. So they employed this mythological framework to express their hope that the grave is not the end. But apart altogether from Scripture, the criticism of the rationalist is perfectly justified here; they are simply producing a religiously garbed version of the old wishful thinking reaction.

But for Paul, and for the believer, the resurrection of Christ is not a mythological statement in which he hopes to find the kernel of some religious truth. It is solid history. It actually happened. There was a lifeless body taken from a cross and laid in a tomb. There was a miracle. The Lord truly rose and there is a list of witnesses cited by Paul to corroborate the fact. That is surely one reason why Paul makes the burial of Christ one distinct element in his gospel, along with the cross and the resurrection, for it was the burial which emphasised beyond all shadow of doubt that it was not a case of someone in a comatose condition who was later resuscitated. The prolonged period in the tomb after the shock and loss of blood of crucifixion makes any talk of a coma quite ridiculous. He really died and He truly arose.

Nor can it be claimed that the disciples were so keyed up with their hopes of His survival that they persuaded themselves that He was alive. Unless we accuse the evangelists of an incredibly clever piece of deceptive writing, we are compelled to acknowledge the evidence of the narratives that the disciples were utterly numbed with shock at the death of Christ and cherished no hope whatever of seeing him again. The comment of the two on the Emmaus road outlines the pathos of their hopelessness: "We trusted that it had been He which should have redeemed Israel." One can feel the underlying sadness in the implicit admission that their hopes had been rudely shattered.

Nor can one dismiss the evidence of the empty tomb. If the story of the resurrection was a pious fabrication why did the Jewish leaders, whose position was undermined by this preaching, not produce the evidence of the corpse? Perhaps the disciples had stolen it? This imposes too much on our credulity! Would men be prepared, as they were, to face torture and death for what they knew to be a fraudulent theory? Would men base the ethical preaching of the New Testament on a blatant lie? Indeed, we must go further still and say that the change from the cowed and demoralised group after the crucifixion, to the confident witnesses after the resurrection, is inexplicable apart from the fact that it really happened. Truly it did, says Paul, and here is witness after witness, many of them still alive at the time of writing, and so able to challenge him. Christ died and rose and lives.

I have spent time on this issue of whether the resurrection is a fact or not, because upon this rests all our hopes not only for this life but for the life to come. Because He rose there is a glory which transforms even the ugliness of death. So, like Paul, we can mock death: "O death where is thy sting. O grave where is thy victory. The sting of death is sin and the strength of sin is the law, but thanks be to God which giveth us the victory through our Lord Jesus Christ" (1 Co. 15: 55-57). The praise of the Church of God down more than nineteen centuries, the joyful testimony of the long line of martyrs, the quiet assurance of an innumerable company of unrecorded lives – all these are rooted in one basic fact, that "Christ is risen from the dead and become the first-fruits of them that slept" (1 Co. 15: 20).

That is why the Christian hope for the future is so rich. We do not believe in some idea of shadowy survival beyond the grave. We are not limited to the old Greek notion of the immortality of the soul. We believe in the resurrection of the body. Death means the tearing asunder of a divinely created unity between soul and body. The body left in its lifeless state returns to dust, but the soul lives on. So, says the apostle, to be "absent from the body" is to be "present with the Lord". That means that death for the Christian is the moment of translation to the presence of Christ. "To depart," writes Paul, is "to be with Christ which is far better" (Ph. 1: 23). So, we hear the triumphant shout from heaven: "I heard a voice from heaven saying unto me, Write, Blessed are the dead which die in the Lord from henceforth. Yea saith the Spirit that they may rest from their labours" (Rev. 14: 13).

But this is not the final vision, for, although it is glorious to contemplate being in the presence of the Lord, there is an even richer hope. While Paul looks forward with joy to being with Christ, it is not to what he calls an "unclothed" condition, but to one in which he is "clothed upon with our house which is from heaven" (2 Co. 5: 2). The biblical view of the body is far removed from the pagan notion that it is the prison-house of the soul from which our only hope is to be set free. When God created man He made him as a unity of soul and body. It is through our bodily life that we express the life of the soul. It is through our bodies that we come into relationships with our fellows. So the biblical hope of the resurrection is an assertion of a continuance of a full personal existence in which the glorified soul has a perfected instrument, the resurrected body, for the expression of the new heavenly life.

This is not to be misconstrued as some kind of reassembly process of a body which in the cycle of nature has long since become a constituent of other bodies. The resurrection body is the product of the supernatural power of God Almighty. In the great chapter on the resurrection of the body Paul uses an illustration from the harvest field. A piece of grain in the spring is bare and dull. To throw it into the ground seems a prescription for destruction, and indeed this is partially true, for the husk rots away. But the living germ survives and sprouts into renewed life. Between the bare seed sown earlier, and the glorious head of grain at harvest, there is a marked contrast, and yet there is also a continuity of life. So the Christian looks forward, not only to a personal continuity in heaven, but also to the great transforming contrast when the body of our humiliation shall be changed into a glorious body akin to that of the exalted Saviour (Ph. 3: 21).

Our enjoyment of life here is affected not only by our bodily health, but by the nature of our environment. It is much more pleasant to live in a suburban village than in a decaying inner city slum. So, too, the Bible speaks of a renewed environment. Not only does the glorified believer enjoy the freedom from sinful weakness because of the perfection of His resurrection body, he also revels in the sublimely perfect environment with no hindrance to his enjoyment. "We look for new heavens and a new earth, wherein dwelleth righteousness" (2 Pe. 3: 13). It is an environment free from sin and so free from all the ugly and grief-laden consequences of sin: "And God shall wipe away all tears from their eyes; and there shall be no more death, neither sorrow, nor crying, neither shall there be any more pain: for the former things are passed away" (Rev. 21: 4).

Heaven and joy are two words which belong together. The illustrations which Jesus used in His parables highlight the joy of the coming day; it is presented in terms of a feast and especially of a wedding feast. Similarly, in the Apocalypse there is a constant upsurge of music. The choir of heaven and the instrumental accompaniment rise to a crescendo of joyful praise as they adore and worship God, and sing the praises of the Lamb. Here our deepest joys always have an underlying pain, for at best they are fleeting, and all too often are tinged with some regret – either due to our past failures or to the absence of someone whose presence would have enhanced our joy. But heaven's joy is not like a sky where clouds begin to gather and shut out the warm brightness of the sun. There is a joy untarnished by selfishness or pride. It is a joy whose permanence rules out any lingering fear of disillusionment to come. It is unlike earth's delights, which when indulged too much become flat and insipid, for in the joy of heaven "there are pleasures for evermore" (Ps. 16: 11).

The supreme joy of heaven is the vision of God Himself. The resurrection of the body and the perfection of heaven are simply the perfect means adapted to this great end. Job, in the midst of his pain, could yet lift his eyes to that great day: "Yet in my flesh shall I see God" (Jb. 19: 26). Jesus pronounced His word "blessed" or "happy" over those "who are pure in heart for they shall see God" (Mt. 5: 8). John in his first epistle sees that vision as the means of our final transformation, "When we shall see Him we shall be like Him for we shall see Him as He is" (1 Jn. 3: 2). Here is an echo of the Psalmist's aspiration which is the confident assurance of all the people of God: "As for me, I will behold Thy face in righteousness: I shall be satisfied, when I awake, with Thy likeness" (Ps. 17: 15).

"Our fellowship is with the Father and with His son Jesus Christ" (1 Jn. 1: 3). That is true now, but in heaven it is fully realised. Then we shall see the Father in all the perfections of His wisdom, love and mercy, and we shall also enjoy a perfect communion with Christ. So Jesus prays for His apostles, and for all who will believe on Him through the apostolic testimony: "Father, I will that they also, whom Thou hast given Me, be with Me where I am; that they may behold My glory, which Thou hast given Me: for Thou lovedst Me before the foundation of the world" (Jn. 17: 24). Robert Traill, the seventeenth-century Puritan, has some telling comments on this prayer of Christ: "Learn to pray moderately for the lives of Christ's people ... who can tell, but Christ and we are praying counter to one another? He may be saying in heaven, 'Father, I will have such a one to be with Me where I am'; and we saying on earth, 'Lord, we would have him to be with us where we are'; we saying, 'We cannot spare him as yet'; and Christ saying, 'I will be no longer without him'. It is the force of this prayer of Christ, 'I will have them to be with me where I am', that is the cause of the death of the godly."[1]

While the supreme joy of heaven is the undisturbed vision of the glory of the Lord – we shall see Him "face to face" (1 Co. 13: 12) – yet there is also the prospect of meeting with, and enjoying fellowship with the people of God. One of the questions which is often asked by those who know the loneliness of bereavement is: "Shall we know one another in heaven?" The answer to that question seems to me to be quite definitely "Yes". For one thing, if there were no continuity of life between here and hereafter, the very idea of resurrection would be virtually robbed of meaning, for heaven would be more akin to the birth or the creation of a new race of people, with no links with the past. But the inhabitants of heaven will be essentially the same people as those who were on earth; transformed, it is true, into Christ's likeness, but still identifiably the same people.

There is further evidence in Scripture to support the hope that we shall recognize and be recognized. When Jesus spoke of the great fellowship sitting down with Abraham, Isaac and Jacob in the kingdom of heaven (Mt. 8: 11), He was surely not employing those names as mere symbols. To a Jewish audience these names were clearly those of the patriarchs who were now in the presence of God. Then, again, in the sombre story of Dives and Lazarus, Jesus pictures Lazarus after death in conscious enjoyment of fellowship with Abraham. But the latter is no mere symbolic figure. He is a real person and is recognized and identified by name as Dives, who from his place of torment also recognizes Lazarus. Hence, when in 1 Thessalonians 4: 13-18 Paul gives his great picture of the triumphant return of the Lord, he speaks of those alive at the coming of Christ being caught up together with those raised from the dead. This is no amorphous mass of undifferentiated humanity, but a warm rich fellowship of people who, in the joy of conscious communion with each other, rejoice in the greater delight of communion with God Himself.

77

Here is comfort for the sorrowing. Here is encouragement for the discouraged. Here is strength for those who are finding the going hard. Listen to the response of the apostle Paul as he contrasts the trials and sorrows and pains of the present with the surpassing glory of the future. "Our light affliction, which is but for a moment, worketh for us a far more exceeding and eternal weight of glory: while we look not at the things which are seen, but at the things which are not seen: for the things which are seen are temporal; but the things which are not seen are eternal" (2 Co. 4: 17-18). "I reckon that the sufferings of this present time are not worthy to be compared with the glory which shall be revealed in us" (Ro. 8: 18). But listen now to Paul's Saviour and Lord. "Let not your hearts be troubled: believe in God believe also in me. In my Father's house are many mansions . . . I go to prepare a place for you, and if I go and prepare a place for you, I will come again and receive you unto myself; that where I am there ye may be also" (Jn. 14: 1-3). To all this there is only one appropriate reply: "Even so, come, Lord Jesus" (Rev. 22: 20).

[1] *The Works of Robert Traill*, Vol. 2, p. 57.

Chapter 10

MENTAL AND PHYSICAL HANDICAP

How can anyone who has not himself suffered the continuing agony of being personally involved with mental or physical handicap write on this most painful subject? He must turn to those who have themselves lived with the situation of having a handicapped child. Indeed it is only because a number of parents were ready to share their own anguished reactions with me that I have even dared to attempt to write this chapter. It represents not so much my views as my distillation of the reflections of those who have faced, or are still facing the heavy responsibility of caring for a handicapped son or daughter.

If there is more emphasis in what follows on the problem of mental handicap, this is in no sense to minimise the pain of physical disability. Indeed at one point one can see in the latter an even wider spread of pain in that it is not only the parents who suffer but also the physically handicapped child or adult. To have a clear mind allied to a sadly defective body is to be acutely aware of one's deprived condition of life. To be able to think deeply is not only to face the constant frustration, but also to be aware of the reactions of others, their pity or their apathy, and to suffer all the more. Yet, at the same time, the clarity of mind which intensifies the pain of the physically handicapped is, by a merciful paradox, the instrument which enables them to adjust to their circumstances and, in very many cases, to develop a range of interests and activities which puts to shame those of us who neglect or abuse the precious gift of a healthy body.

Because the two conditions have many features in common much of this chapter applies to both. In a sense, what is more specifically applicable to mental handicap serves to highlight the general condition in that it focuses thought not only on the handicapped person himself, but also on the parents and the other members of the family who share the pain. They will find much of what is written here only too familiar – after all, they live with the situation every day. But then a major reason for writing the chapter is not to tell such sufferers what they already know, but to arouse others to a sympathetic awareness of the problem. If I succeed in doing this I will have in some measure discharged my debt to the parents who have bared their own souls. At least it will show them that I have been greatly moved by what they wrote. I can only hope that some echo of that may be heard by others.

A major problem for parents is the sense of loneliness and isolation. So many friends, even their Christian friends, seem to be unconcerned or to have only a very superficial sympathy. To face a desperate and unending struggle is bad enough; to face it all alone is even worse. The feeling of a complete lack of understanding on the part of others can be intensified by the glib replies they make. From the non-Christian it is the "cheer up" type of advice; from the Christian it is an equally glib approach in which a text is tossed to the sufferer as if such a passing concern could provide any real help.

The sense of isolation can be deepened by the unqualified cheerfulness of the shallowly optimistic who predict improvement in the future, when a parent knows with a numbing certainty that the condition will not improve, but is more likely to grow worse. In some cases they themselves entertained such a hope. They can recall the dawning realisation that something was wrong with their baby. Then came the prolonged agony of being tormented by false hopes either of improvement or of some medical break-through. But such dreams ebbed into the bleak realisation that the condition would never improve. The blandly expressed expectations for the future proffered by some well wisher do no more than open the old wounds of disappointed hopes.

In the case of mental handicap the reaction of others can be even more painful. People clearly have a fear of any kind of mental defect or illness. It is noticeable for example that people will very readily visit friends or neighbours who are in a general hospital; they are on familiar ground and can often discuss their own experiences of major surgery, but in the case of the psychiatric hospital it is usually only the loyal relative who persists in visiting, and even members of the family can be reluctant to go. Diabetes or gallstones they can in some measure understand, but psychiatric illness leaves them uncertain and fearful. This same fear leads many simply to avoid the handicapped and this avoidance not only wounds the feelings but deepens the loneliness.

There are still those who tend to see such a handicap as evidence of hidden sinfulness on the part of the parents. Indeed some parents themselves succumb to this notion and torture themselves with self-accusations. They feel a deep shame that they have brought such a child into the world, and allied to that shame is a feeling of guilt that in some, perhaps indefinable, way they are partly to blame. If such parents are Christians they will find one critic at least who will delight to deepen their misery. The devil is well called "the accuser of the brethren". He will insinuate into the turmoil of soul the vicious suggestion that maybe there is some truth in the idea after all. The only answer to this monstrous untruth which can so intensify their pain is to go back to the book of Job, or to listen to Jesus as He rejects out of hand the specious idea that the blind man was suffering either for his own sins or for the sins of his parents.

Work is one of God's blessings to men and the inevitable toil of looking after a child is one of the laborious joys of a young mother. But much as she loves her baby and much as she enjoys caring for him she still breathes a sigh of relief when her husband arrives home to help. While small children are a delight, it is still a great moment when they are safely off to bed and husband and wife can relax. In any case those days of seemingly unending toil are simply one stage and soon toddlers become less demanding – that is unless they are severely handicapped. Here is where the gladly accepted care of a child so easily slips into the grim drudgery which never seems to end. When the mentally handicapped child or young adult is physically active it becomes an even more wearing experience, demanding much both of physical and emotional energy. Indeed it is so demanding that, with the daily burden and the prospect of a permanent future commitment, the resources can be so drained that the parents feel themselves at times on the edge of despair.

If there are other healthy children in the family there are further problems. It is true that they can be a great help in the constant task of caring for the handicapped member, but there is the uneasy feeling of the parents that the others are being penalised in various ways. They may be restricted in the outings they can enjoy or the holidays they can take. The heavy additional expenses involved in their situation can produce financial pressures which in turn mean children being denied what many of their fellows take for granted. Then, too, some children can be very sensitive and they have to face the other children who can be savage in their unkindness and in their contemptuous attitude to the disabled.

On the credit side of this particular problem is the fact that children with a handicapped brother or sister are being trained in the school of sympathy. Their lessons are not learned from books but from the strains and tears and frustrations of a family life which has been distorted by tragedy. Yet when this tragedy is rightly used it can become the instrument for teaching them a concern for others, a thankful appreciation of their own healthy bodies and minds, and a willingness to sacrifice oneself for the good of others. Graduates from this kind of academy of pain have qualifications which no course on social concern could ever confer.

The outsider who can only see a handicapped child as a burden cannot easily grasp how deeply parents can love such a child. The very struggle to care for the child day and night over the years can weld the normal love of a parent into something even deeper because of the inevitable protective role involved in the relationship. But this very protectiveness can bring further problems. There is the danger of becoming aggressive with others and of seeing education or hospital agencies as totally lacking in understanding. It can lead also to a state of anxious tension which at times makes normal relationships with outsiders difficult and even prayer becomes a struggle.

A further pain in this love for a handicapped child is the resentment at the unthinking attitude of others. To the latter the child is an example of a particular kind of defect. He is a spastic or a mongol. But to the parent he is no more a statistic than any other child. He is a person who, with all his deficiencies of body or of mind, has his own individuality. How hurtful it is to find their child treated in an impersonal way as if he or she were a thing rather than a person. This kind of attitude is seen in the way people do not address the child directly, even though in the case of physical handicap he is perfectly able to understand and to reply. One does not normally ask a parent whether the child takes sugar in his tea or wants a sweet – one asks the child. Why then should the handicapped child be treated as if he had no individuality at all? When the handicapped child has grown to manhood or womanhood it adds insult to injury to approach them in this indirect fashion as if they were some peculiar species needing an interpreter. In some severe cases they may in fact need such, but it is better to begin where the Bible begins, which is to treat each person as an individual in his own rights and not simply as an appendage of others.

All the time there is the nagging fear at the back of the mind: "What about the future?" In the past many handicapped people tended to die young so that they were under the care of their parents throughout their brief life. Now, however, they can survive the difficult years of adolescence and may well outlive their parents. For the Christian parent, who has lavished love and care on a child and then on the mature adult, it is agony to think of leaving that one behind to the care of some state institution. For one whose handicap has been in some measure counter-balanced by the protection and security of a Christian home, the possibility of ending life in the care of those who, with all their concern for physical well being, have none at all for spiritual issues – this is a sad prospect for any Christian parent.

Are there any answers to these most agonising problems? Some have been suggested earlier in this book. There is the realisation that we live in a fallen world where the discordant condition of creation brings in its train all the varied pains and sufferings to which men fall heir. There is the awareness that God is our heavenly father caring for us in the darkest hours. There is the assurance that the Saviour who watches over His handicapped disciples is a sympathetic friend. But clearly each parent has to apply these truths to his or her own particular situation. There will be many a struggle of soul as the mind wrestles with its questionings, and as at times the resentment wells up that other people should have healthy children and normal lives. Yet it is in submission to the providence of God that peace is found. It is in acceptance of His will that the only secure foundation for weathering the storms is to be found.

One parent with a severely handicapped son wrote in his letter of this kind of attitude: "I think that the greatest issue is the acceptance of God's will. Once this is granted everything else falls into place and daily help is found. At first this was not simple. The Lord had given him to us. Why does a loving omnipotent God choose to make such a gift suffer from defects when at a word He is able to remove them? In acceptance there is peace. This is the outstanding issue, a willingness to own that our understanding of His love does not rest upon our understanding of His dealing with us!"

The same parent added some wise words on prayer gleaned from his own and his wife's suffering: "One issue concerns the very nature of prayer. This has to be the acceptance of His will. To struggle against this can easily be selfish defiance and even a wish to dictate to Him. There is so much unbiblical and extreme teaching today that I feel many must find this a problem. Verses can be taken out of their context and made to serve a false view of suffering and even of the atonement. Then, when disappointment follows, faith can be lost. I feel very much for those who have been told that their weak faith is the reason for the continued suffering of their loved one. This is a grievous effect of shallow views of the whole problem."

All this has to do with the parents of handicapped children. But they are not the only ones who need to learn lessons. The church at large needs to learn them. Indeed most of us are in more acute need of learning, for often we have not begun to realise our own ignorance in this area, and need to be jolted out of our insensitivity. We need to learn the sympathy of the Lord. We need to appreciate what it means to "weep with those who weep". Such sympathy will not be of the effusive kind which only hurts the sufferers more by singling them out as objects of pity. Nor is it to be at the level of mere words. It must also involve action. In a local church where handicap is a fact of the actual situation, practical concern is needed: the offer of hospitality for a handicapped child for a few days to give the parents a break; the invitation to the handicapped person himself to share a meal. Here are obvious actions and there are others which can soon be discovered. Neither the handicapped nor their parents require pity but they desperately need love. May God forgive us for being so blind to their needs.

Let me end with two illustrations which bring their own moving appeal. The first one concerns a trio out for a walk in the country – two parents and their handicapped child. It is the kind of situation where, away from a crowded street, one can exchange a brief word. In this case the initiative came from a Christian whom they met. He made some friendly comment about their little girl, the kind of remark that is so normal. But in this case the effect was immediate. The parents broke down in tears. No one ever took notice of their child. Other parents might have the pleasure of hearing their child being commented on for winning a prize or passing an exam or even having a pretty dress. But their child, in her handicap, was virtually a non-person to others. To find someone taking notice of their little girl and seeing worth in their child was an overwhelming experience.

The other incident comes from a university situation. This is the context of stirring appeals for the under-privileged and demonstrations on behalf of the oppressed. But far eclipsing these usual features of student life was a remarkable demonstration of Christian love. The student in question was very severely handicapped with physical disabilities which made it imperative that in feeding and even in toilet requirements he had to have assistance. Such a man surely could not face a university course. But he did, and showed marked ability. Behind his achievement, however, was the selfless attitude of Christian students who accepted the responsibility of caring for him in all his desperate weakness. The university authorities, who would only enroll him on condition that someone should be responsible for him, saw in action a Christianity not buttressed by clever arguments but powerfully reinforced by loving service. I can hear the Lord say, "Go and do thou likewise".

CHAPTER 11

UNHAPPY MARRIAGE

To put the pain of an unhappy marriage in the same bracket as the suffering of prolonged illness, or the sorrow of bereavement, may seem to some to be a serious over-statement. They will admit that it is a very painful experience, but they will claim that it is not really so overwhelming, and in any case it can be terminated by a divorce. Such an objector can never have known at first hand the misery of such a shattered relationship. He must never have seen the effects in the lives of the children who are the victims of a marital split. Indeed to talk glibly of a divorce terminating it all is like saying that the problem of a badly smashed leg in an accident can quickly be settled by an amputation. Radical surgery may be the only answer to a desperate situation but it leaves many other problems in its wake.

After some thirty-two years as a minister of the Word, during which time it has been on occasions my painful responsibility to try and bring healing to troubled marriages, it is my considered judgement that some of the greatest mental agony I have witnessed has been in this area. A small study armchair of mine is a mute witness to such anguish, with a deep mark where someone distraught with grief quite unconsciously dug a finger nail into the wood.

Indeed I would go so far as to say that in some ways a broken marriage is a far more bitter grief than even the crushing sorrow of bereavement. This is not in any way to minimise bereavement, for it is a quite devastating experience. To lose a loved partner through death is to be left with memories which, though they bring pain, also by their sweetness bring some solace, but to lose a partner through adultery or desertion is to face the same kind of loneliness as bereavement, but with memories whose bitterness makes the loneliness even more acute.

In many cases there is no final breach. A couple will often stay together for the sake of the children, by which time the open hostility of the past may have given way to a grimly resigned mutual tolerance. But the condition is at best drab and wretched, and at worst unbearably agonising.

Yet, in the majority of cases, the two who are now so bitterly estranged believed they were deeply in love. Few people surely enter marriage with the intention of making shipwreck of their relationship. They know that many marriages do end on the rocks, but they are sure that theirs could not possibly be in that sad category. They intend that theirs shall succeed where others have failed. Yet again and again it is the same story of mutual misunderstanding, of petty issues inflated to major proportions, of mistrust and bitter recriminations and angry quarrels, and finally the inevitable break-up.

Nor is the agony confined to the two chief participants. There is no more pathetic victim than the child who is torn asunder by his affection for both his parents, when he is forced by reasons beyond his control, and possibly even beyond his comprehension, to live with one parent, when he does not want to leave the other. One of the most moving answers to any question is that of the child being forced to say which parent he wishes to live with. His reply will not satisfy the demands of a court which must make some kind of settlement, but it is the natural though tragic cry of a child's heart; he does not want to live with his father or his mother; he wants them both.

The child's tragedy is that he is not only deprived of what is his birthright, the care of both his parents, but sometimes he becomes the victim of the jealousy and spite of his parents. I recall a case where the father had been given regular access to his son. I felt that he was only making use of the access to maintain his rights, and possibly to spite his wife. Of any sign of affection for the son there was none. The boy's misery was quite heart-breaking.

It is true that in bereavement also, a child is deprived of a father or a mother, but it is a very different situation. His memory is of two parents who loved one another deeply. Death has cruelly cut short that relationship and deprived him of a greatly loved parent. He feels the loss deeply, and will continue to feel it, but he does not have the bitter memories of a father and mother fiercely opposed to each other. His sorrow may be very deep, but the very fact that a sorrowing parent is also mourning the loss means that they can share together. That comfort, however, is denied to the child of the broken home. His bewildered pain leaves scars which may take years to heal, if indeed there is ever complete healing.

It comes as something of a shock to some people to realise that Christians are not immune from the tragedy of a marriage breakdown. Indeed, their pain can be all the greater because they have such a high ideal for marriage. They do not subscribe to the modern pattern of unchastity before marriage, unfaithfulness after, and a separation or divorce as an option to keep open. They believe in marriage as an ordinance given by God; a lifelong union between one man and one woman. They repudiate the notion of any competing relationship with someone else. They believe too in the grace of God to meet their problems. Yet they may face the awful realisation that their marriage seems to be heading in the same direction as that of some acquaintances who are not Christians at all.

One must ask why there are such break-downs between Christians. It is not a rather sad question by way of conducting some kind of post-mortem. It is rather an insistent question which requires answers, for it concerns not only those who need help in their marriage relationship, but young Christians who are contemplating marriage. They need to realise that marriage is not an automatic success. Of course one does not need to go to the other absurd extreme of suggesting that only a few will make the grade, for, in fact, in my experience, the majority of Christian marriages are happy ones. But because of the substantial minority which are not, and because we want to warn young Christians of the pitfalls, we need to ask how it is that a Christian couple can end in a marriage break-down.

In some cases it can be due to the fact that one partner never was a Christian at all. Love is blind and never more so than when a relationship is maturing, and marriage begins to be more than an exciting possibility. Naturally the two involved will want to avoid whatever jars upon the other. They will be keen to show where they have common interests. A similar outlook on life will be seen as an important asset. In this situation it is very easy for a non-Christian to produce a profession of faith which may be accepted as real, but is in fact quite spurious. It is not necessarily a case of deliberate hypocrisy. The wish is father to the thought, and a fellow who desperately wants to marry a Christian girl may persuade not only her, but himself, that he is a true believer. When the inevitable stresses and strains of marriage come, the spurious profession will be seen for what it really is – and what perhaps it always was for the discerning Christian friends, who tried to dissuade the Christian partner, but whose advice was not heeded.

On the other hand, they may both have been true believers when they married. Indeed their early marriage may have been not only very happy as far as they themselves were concerned, but very fruitful in the work of the church and the service of the gospel. Then one of them begins to drift spiritually. Backsliding does not happen overnight. It often begins in a growing slackness in prayer, or a lack of discipline in Christian living. Imperceptibly the Christian begins to move outside the orbit of the church. With new friends come new tastes and habits. The slope becomes increasingly steep until he or she is in a condition which they would once have thought inconceivable. To the husband or wife who remains steady in their Christian living, and whose great aim is to press on in holiness and in service for Christ, the change can be agonising. No longer do they pray together. Mutual discussion of the things of God becomes a memory. To the Christian the grief is intense.

There is a further reason for the break-up of Christian marriages, and, though it may seem strange, it is because they paid attention before their marriage to a basic biblical requirement, but unhappily failed to consider other important factors. The Bible is quite clear: "Be not unequally yoked together with unbelievers." The Christian must never contemplate marriage with an unbeliever. That is the path of disobedience and the high road to disaster. But a couple may both be Christians, and then make the great mistake of thinking that, so long as they have fulfilled this basic requirement, then all is well. While it is certainly vital that they should both be Christians, there are other important elements in a happy and successful marriage. It is one thing to share a common experience of the new birth and a common concern for the work of God. After all, we share these with all our fellow Christians. But marriage is a highly selective step, and it is important to appreciate that such factors as shared interests, basic cultural agreement, generally compatible outlooks are all necessary. True spirituality does not become so ethereal that it ignores the fact that it is not two disembodied spirits who are considering marriage, but two people of flesh and blood.

Turning again to the desperate agony of a marriage break-down, I find it necessary at times to reassure the Christian that it is not wrong to feel the pain deeply. Christians may indeed add to their personal unhappiness by questioning whether in fact they should be so desperately unhappy. They may feel utterly shattered by the blow, when a partner proves unfaithful or simply walks out of the home. They then may torment themselves further by wondering if there is something wrong in this anguished condition. By way of reply I would say, that not only is it completely natural for a person to feel shattered, but in fact it would be most unnatural – and indeed most unspiritual – if he or she did not feel like this. Why then is the pain so deep that even tears are an inadequate expression?

In the first place it is because the very nature of the marriage relationship as God ordained it is that two people should become one flesh. They are united in a sacred bond in which the physical union is closely knit with the total union of their two personalities. They are no longer two but one. When that unity is brutally torn asunder by adultery or desertion, it is inevitable that it will leave torn edges which will not easily heal. In a true marriage two people find their fulfilment in each other. There is a mutual giving and receiving in every area of life, both in the most intimate moments and in the general context of daily living. It is in that mutual interplay that they are enriched, and their personalities develop. With a breakdown comes the awful sense of a desperate emptiness. There is the desire still to give and there is no one there to receive, or else the giving is spurned. There is still the desire to receive, but there is no gift, or worse still, the gifts are seen to be given to another.

Then, again, the mutual help and encouragement which a happy marriage provides are no longer there. One of the great privileges of a stable marriage is to have a partner to whom to turn. A man may be facing great stresses in his work. His day may leave him feeling drained of nervous energy. It is a tremendous strength to be able to come home and either to share some of the burdens with his wife or simply to relax in her company when the tensions of the day can be put to one side. But with a troubled relationship that strengthening home base is no longer there. Indeed it is an even worse situation, for the problems of the working day give way to the even greater tensions of the evening. To try and avoid the latter by going out as much as possible in the evenings does not solve the problem, but merely provides a temporary and unsatisfactory escape.

To compensate for the unhappy home situation by throwing himself into his work, even when his job is a very congenial one, is still only a means of escape, and in the case of a worthwhile job there is not the chance of sharing the enjoyment with an appreciative listener.

With a wife there is a similar burden. She is forced to become both father and mother to her children, either because her husband avoids home as much as possible or because he has finally gone. Bringing up children is a very demanding business, whether it is the sheer physical drudgery of coping with very demanding and at times very wearing toddlers, or whether it is the nervous stresses of facing teenage upheavals. To be able to share the burden makes it lighter. For an over pressed young mother the willing help in the evening is not only a physical relief, but has the added reassurance of a caring attitude from her husband. For both of them to be able to discuss together and pray together in face of the problems of their teenage children is to be able to face those rather turbulent years more easily. But for a young mother to face an evening when the heavy work load of the day gives way to the blank emptiness of a lonely evening is a bleak experience. For one parent to try and deal with a rather rebellious teenager, whose attitude may have been accentuated by his parents' quarrels, this is to face a desperately grievous situation.

In addition to all these pains and stresses, there is the continually nagging doubt: "What did I do wrong? How did we go astray?" In fact the one who asks those questions in the stark emptiness of a broken home, may be largely the innocent victim. It may well be that it is the other partner to the marriage who carries the major responsibility, and the detached judgement of friends or relations may fully confirm this. But this does not always alleviate the pain of the inner questioning. Even admitting the other's guilt, was there a failure in some area? Did the children take up too much of the wife's attention so that she failed to remain the kind of woman he had married? Did the husband become so involved in his work or his sporting activities that his wife felt like a widow? Such lesser failures certainly do not justify the gross betrayal of adultery, but they still leave their pains behind.

There are obvious dangers in the possible reactions to the pain of a broken marriage. There is the natural tendency to self-pity which is a constant human reaction in face of disappointment or suffering. This self-pity can be deepened by the evidence on every hand of deeply united couples, with a stable relationship and an obviously happy family life. Each time the solitary partner goes to church and sees husbands and wives worshipping together, the pain can become worse. School prize days or graduations are again tinged with desperate disappointment, as other young people have two delighted parents, and their own children have one missing. But self-pity is never a healthy response. It shuts a person in with his problems and slams the door firmly on any possible solution. If it is indulged in for long it can produce a bitter and cynical attitude whose hardening effects make the isolation from others almost total.

An allied reaction can be the complaining and querulous attitude where the offended partner can think and speak of nothing but the hurt that has been inflicted. The husband's desertion, the wife's unfaithfulness, the behaviour of the person who came between them, the unsympathetic attitude of in-laws, the indifference of friends – these and a multitude of other petty complaints become the main topic of conversation. It is no wonder if friends find it hard to remain sympathetic. It is no surprise that they seem to be indifferent. It is hard to withstand a non-stop barrage of complaints. Indeed there is the lurking suspicion that this querulous approach may well have been one of the corroding influences in the deterioration of the relationship.

It is important to be able to share the trouble at such a time. This is all the more important in a broken marriage, for the normal confidence is no longer there. To bottle up one's feelings is to compound the difficulty. To have a trusted friend or a wise pastor is a very great help. But there are two words of caution needed. The person with whom things are shared must be one who can keep a confidential matter utterly secret. The hope of rebuilding a broken relationship will not be enhanced if intimate and personal details find their way back to the estranged partner. The other cautionary word concerns the circle of those with whom the problems are shared. It is one thing to share in general terms with a wider circle of friends, it is quite another to recount to all and sundry the misdeeds of the wrongdoer. This certainly is the way to ensure that the breakdown will continue.

It is important to face the situation realistically. If there has been a cooling off in the affections, these cannot be re-heated like a meal being pushed into the oven. A dutiful attitude is no adequate replacement for love which has gone cold. This does not excuse the utterly wrong conclusion, which is often drawn, that there is nothing that can be done, and the only answer is to signal the end of the relationship in the divorce court. There is something that can be done, and that is to maintain faithfulness, and from that basic standpoint to work at the restoration of the marriage. While it is true that a love which has been rejected or deeply hurt cannot easily be re-kindled, it is not true that it can never be restored. But it is important to face the situation in a realistic way and to see that the process of restoration may be slow and at times may encounter disappointing set-backs.

It is at this point that differences of temperament can be seen. One person who is fairly placid may be able to wait hopefully, and to work steadily towards a restoration of life together. Another is of a much more impatient and impetuous disposition, always wanting to get plans settled and details organised. For such a temperament the anxiety to see the marriage restored as soon as possible can in fact make the restoration more difficult. The other partner, whether husband or wife, may be trying to extricate themselves from some other liaison and to return to a faithful relationship. But they cannot simply stir up the affections which have waned, and to try to force the pace can have the opposite effect by putting them on the defensive. To force one partner into a corner of self-justification is to introduce a further element of discord which may greatly impede the path to recovery.

These are practical considerations, not to be despised by an ultra-spirituality which loses touch with the human situation. But clearly there are even more important factors. The Christian is not on his own battling with his grief. Nor is he dependent simply on a circle of close friends, no matter how sympathetic and helpful they may be. He knows the living God as his Father, Christ as his advocate and sympathetic friend, and the Holy Spirit as his indwelling comforter and guide. So he not only attempts to deal responsibly with the situation in terms of practical wisdom, he turns constantly to the God in whom he not only finds wisdom to guide him in the darkness, but strength to keep him going in moments of near despair, and consolation for a sorely bruised spirit.

One of the discoveries here, as in other areas of intense pain, is that the very suffering leads to a deep communion with the Lord. To lose an earthly partner, to be deprived of human love, to have no one with whom to share the problems and burdens, is to be driven back to the realisation that ultimately our hope and our strength are in God. "God is our refuge and strength, a very present help in trouble" (Ps. 46: 1). The very darkness of grief makes the light of the presence of God all the more appealing. The silence of the human voice, or perhaps even worse, the bitter and angry words of an estranged husband or wife, make the gracious invitations of the Lord all the more compelling. When life has narrowed into a distressing cul-de-sac, it is balm to a hurt spirit to hear the Lord calling, "Come unto me all ye that labour and are heavy laden and I will give you rest" (Mt. 11: 28).

Hosea learnt such lessons in his own bitter experience. His wife proved unfaithful and he faced what is one of the greatest agonies of all: knowing that the child she bore was not his. But in those dark hours he learnt lessons which not only lit up his own darkness, but have blessed God's people down the centuries. As he reflected on the ugliness of unfaithfulness, when a husband or wife breaks a sacred covenant and deeply injures the other partner, he began to see the awfulness of Israel's unfaithfulness. God has pledged Himself to His people in the covenant of grace. He has freely forgiven them. He has brought them into relationship with Himself. That covenant relationship has been sealed as authentic by the death of Christ; we recall the Lord's saying, repeated constantly at the Lord's Supper: "This cup is the new covenant in my blood." How grievous then is our unfaithfulness when we break the covenant! How ungrateful we are when we turn from our heavenly lover and embrace the world with its seductive attractions! So Hosea's pain taught him, and still teaches the heart-broken sufferer, that in communion with the Lord true comfort is to be found.

There is a further lesson: the wonder of God's forgiveness. Ugly and foul though our unfaithfulness to the covenant may be, yet He is gracious and ready to forgive and to restore. If God who has been so deeply grieved by our unfaithfulness is ready to forgive, then surely those who have tasted the agony of betrayal must also be ready to forgive. It will not be easy. There will be a struggle with the bitterness which so readily wells up, but the mercy of God will not only set the standard for forgiveness, it will also melt the unforgiving heart.

There is, however, an important qualification. True forgiveness is not a unilateral declaration. There must also be repentance. God Himself does not forgive the sinner who persists in his sins. To declare pardon to such a one would not be forgiveness at all; it would simply be condoning sin. So the husband or wife, who is the innocent victim of the other's unfaithfulness, is not required to

94

forgive a persistently unfaithful partner. Readiness to forgive, and even a willingness to overlook a further lapse – Yes! But where there is no evidence of repentance, and no sign of any attempt at amendment, then it is idle to speak of forgiveness.

Where there is repentance, and where there is forgiveness, it is important that this forgiveness should be allied with trust. When God pardons the sinner He does not hark back to the past. The record is closed and the pardon is final. "As far as the east is from the west, so far hath he removed our transgressions from us" (Ps. 103 : 12). "I have blotted out as a thick cloud thy transgressions and as a cloud thy sins" (Is. 44 : 22). It is sadly true that we find it hard to approach this gracious attitude. It is so easy to revert to past injury. Too often there is an underlying mistrust which, in a sense, is understandable, for past betrayal can leave a deep feeling of insecurity. But such mistrust, especially if it is detected, will tend either to discourage the offender or to drive him or her back with the feeling, "What's the point of trying?" The ministry of forgiveness can be a very exacting one. But then we remember that our own forgiveness is rooted in the supremely costly sacrifice of Calvary.

But what if every attempt at reconciliation fails? What if the unfaithfulness settles into a firm relationship with someone else? What if the break-down becomes final? Well, there are no glib answers for such a grim situation. There is the stark realisation of a lonely future. Life may seem to be utterly in ruins. Yet life must go on, and if there are children their welfare will be a paramount consideration. The days ahead must be faced. There must be a resolute determination to rebuild a shattered life.

All this may sound like extremely cold comfort, or an impossibly difficult assignment. Then we go back to the prophecy of Hosea. Out of his deep agony God brought great blessing. The dark night in his soul has proved to be the dawning day for many who have read his prophecy. But if you should be in his situation, remember that Hosea's God is your God. Your partner may have forsaken and betrayed you, but your God will never leave you. The way ahead may be intolerably painful, and at times, the mists of doubt and fear may cloud the path, but "the eternal God is thy refuge, and underneath are the everlasting arms" (De. 33 : 27). Even in this situation "God is able to make all grace abound" (2 Co. 9 : 8). In your loneliness it remains true, and it will always remain true: "I will never leave thee nor forsake thee" (He. 13 : 5).

CHAPTER 12

DEPRESSION

A major feature of medical care today is the psychiatric hospital, and a major product of the pharmaceutical industry is the tranquilliser. The reason is not far to seek; it is the very widespread incidence of depression, a condition which is much more common than many people realise. One reason for the unawareness of the magnitude of the problem is that often it is only the tip of the iceberg which is visible. Very many people are slow to display their inner feelings openly. They do not wear their heart on their sleeve, and their hidden fears and anxieties remain concealed. With some it is due to a reluctance to burden other people, and with others it is because of a feeling of shame over what they judge to be their own failure to cope with their personal problems. As a result, they live troubled lives behind a facade which they try to maintain in public, but which is far removed from their real condition.

While the attempt to keep the difficulty to oneself is understandable it leaves the sufferer with two further problems. In the first place, his depression is liable to be deepened by the constant attempt to cover it up. We are gregarious creatures, and the natural instinct is to share freely with one another. If we are constantly trying to bottle up our feelings and to exhibit a cheerful face to the world, we are liable to accentuate the condition so that when the breaking point comes the situation can be much worse than it might have been had it been faced openly at a much earlier stage. This is not to advocate the opposite extreme of confronting everyone at large with our personal problems, but simply to indicate the danger of constant repression of feelings which cry out from the depths for outward expression.

An allied problem emerging from this attempt to cover up a troubled mind with a cheerful face, is that we deprive ourselves of the counsel and help which we may so desperately need. Many of our friends may have little experience of dealing with other people's problems, so that they may take our cheerfulness at its face value and assume that we find life quite straightforward. If they themselves have perplexing difficulties of one kind or another, they are even more liable to overlook our situation. Some who may be more discerning, and who, perhaps, from their own experience, recognise the brave attempt to hide the inner stress, may feel they do not know us well enough to raise the matter. Their reluctance to intrude in what is a very personal area of life may leave them silent, when we desperately need someone to speak to us – or perhaps, even more important, someone to listen to us.

Clearly the intensity of depression varies very greatly from one individual to another. For many it is a sporadic experience, and may be only short lived. But for others it is a constantly recurring problem, and can indeed become virtually a permanent condition. For one it is like a black cloud on a summer day, blotting out the sunshine, unpleasant while it lasts, but mercifully of fairly short duration. For another it is like a really bad summer in which the sun appears fitfully in a constantly overcast sky, as one atmospheric depression is quickly followed by another. But whether of short duration or prolonged in character, depression is the experience of a great many people including, unfortunately, many Christians.

It is important to note at the outset that there are various factors which may enter into what is a very complex condition. Not all of these will be present in every case in the same proportion or to the same degree. We shall begin therefore with general considerations. Afterwards we shall turn to more specific and individual issues, before attempting to formulate answers which deal with the heart of the problem, rather than merely skating on the surface.

There is, in the first place, the factor which is all too often over-looked by Christians, namely, the physical. In their readiness to find a spiritual solution to their problems, they forget that sometimes there is a bodily need which requires attention. A sinner certainly needs the gospel, but if he is starving he also requires food, and indeed if we leave him unfed he will find it hard to concentrate on what we are saying to him. So, while it is true that we must ultimately lead the depressed person to the great physician of the soul, Christ himself, we must also ascertain if there is some bodily need to be met.

It does not require much thought or experience to notice that certain bodily conditions have a depressing effect on us. The most cheerful extrovert can find the aftermath of influenza producing a strangely dampening effect on his normally buoyant temperament. The slow convalescence after major surgery can also produce a depressed condition, as the return to normal vigorous living seems at times to be indefinitely delayed. Childbirth leads to the overwhelming joy of having a long awaited baby, but it has also been the prelude for many a young mother to a different kind of travail, that of post-natal depression. To give one further example, a time of excessive overwork can lead not only to physical breakdown but to such a drain of nervous energy that the outcome is severe depression.

To emphasise the physical factor is not to ignore the spiritual side. Indeed there may be spiritual failure to be exposed even in the physical condition. Thus, the strain of overwork may be due to the neglect of the principle of a weekly rest day so firmly laid down in the Bible in the Sabbath ordinance. If a man flagrantly ignores this he need not expect anything but trouble. Ministers of the Gospel are perhaps especially vulnerable here. For them the Lord's Day is not exactly a rest day as it is for the congregation, in the sense of being a respite from the normal demands. In fact for them those demands reach a climax in the mentally and nervously exhausting task of preaching, not to mention the spiritual conflict involved. If, then, they continue without any break from week to week, they should not be surprised to discover that Sabbath observance is an ordinance built into the basic necessity of man's constitution. The stress resulting from ignoring this can build up until there is a nervous collapse.

But there is a further reason for noting the physical factor in depression, apart from the practical conclusions of prescribing rest or medical treatment for some obvious conditions. It is that by ignoring their bodies, and the effect of bodily states on their minds, Christians especially are liable to exacerbate their condition. They assume too quickly that there must be some serious spiritual failure to explain their depression, and as a result they castigate themselves without necessarily touching the real problem. The devil will of course be delighted to assist them here. As the "accuser of the brethren" he is always ready to twist a rightly sensitive conscience into one which becomes morbid. So the unhappy Christian searches his mind to find some unconfessed sin. He prays to the Lord to show him his sin and his disobedience, and when the Lord does not lay His finger on some such wilful sin the Christian continues his own unrelenting self scrutiny. There is a self-examination which is desirable and profitable, but this dissection of the soul is pathological and plunges the Christian into a complete morass of perplexity. While he continues to twist and turn, probing his conscience and scouring his memory, it may be that he is requiring medical care or simply a period of complete rest.

Turning from the physical side we must notice also the bearing of temperamental factors. We are different the one from the other, not only in our facial appearance or intellectual ability but also in our temperament. Once again too many Christians ignore this temperamental factor when it should be in view from the very outset. The reason for ignoring it can, at least in some cases, be traced to their faulty view of the nature of the new birth. This in turn stems from the kind of evangelism which has been current for a long time, in which the evangelistic techniques have been so well ordered, and the procedure of decision making so standardised, that converts emerge like stereotypes off an assembly line. But in reality they are not stereotypes. They have been fitted into a certain mould and they condition themselves to think of being a certain kind of person, but in fact they are, deep down, as varied as ever. The God who created us with all the rich diversity of personality does not run counter to His own designs when He regenerates the sinner. He is not like the assembly line worker. He is rather the skilled craftsman producing with consummate care each individual product as an evidence of His skill, His wisdom, and His own concern. We do not acquire different facial features when we are born again, no more do we acquire a new temperament. What we do receive is the life of God in our souls, so that while formerly we were controlled by our temperament, now, by the grace of God, we begin to control it. The "old man" simply went the way his temperament led him, whereas the "new man" directs it by the power of the indwelling Holy Spirit. But the born again believer still has the temperament with which he was born and with which he will die.

While there is an infinite variety of human types, we can detect two broad groupings. Like any such classification, a qualification is required in that the dividing lines are not sharply drawn. Hence, the features of one group may be seen much more markedly in one individual than another, and others again may seem in some ways to straddle the dividing line. But with this qualifying consideration we may still recognise the two main groupings of introverts and extroverts.

The introvert, as the name suggests, is one who is inclined to turn inwards on himself, while the extrovert readily turns towards others. Thus the extrovert tends to be "hail fellow well met". He is outgoing and active, and tends to be a cheerful, or at least a fairly sanguine person. The introvert, by contrast, tends to be cautious, not because he lacks courage but because he will examine himself and analyse his motives and his aims. As a result he can become morbidly introspective with an obsessive concern with himself. Because of his temperament he is obviously much more liable to become depressed. But before the extrovert begins to feel superior he needs to take heed to himself. If the introvert's danger is that of becoming over scrupulous, his is at the other extreme, that of becoming shallow and superficial. In other words, an awareness of our own particular temperament is vital to all of us, for we then see the kind of weakness to which we are especially prone and the precautions we must therefore be careful to take. For an introvert to appreciate his tendency to excessive self-analysis is to be on his guard. He will still wish to maintain a healthy attitude of self-examination, but he will be alert for the symptoms of a hyper-sensitive conscience. It is good after all for a shop-keeper to take stock regularly, but if he does nothing else but take stock he will end in bankruptcy.

The Christian will not however rest with a consideration of the physical and temperamental factors, important though these are. He will obviously be alive to other practical issues such as particular tensions which may be alleviated, or of tangled relationships which need to be put right. But above and beyond all these he will be asking questions about the spiritual factors. Indeed that is one reason why a non-Christian psychiatrist may fail completely to understand his needs. To him the spiritual issues are to be explained as a pathological condition which is to be resolved by finding some means of clearing up a guilt complex, or dissolving some scruple which in the non-Christian's view stands in the way of mental liberation. I recall trying to help a young man who had followed the disastrous advice of such a non-Christian psychiatrist to have an affair, and so presumably to overcome his moral scruples which were allegedly the cause of the trouble. The tragic consequence was not only moral failure but utter confusion of mind.

But in taking the spiritual aspect of the problem seriously, the Christian has to be very careful, for while it is true that his faith will be the great means of his deliverance, it can, in a paradoxical way, add to his problems. Because he is a Christian he tries to view the whole of life from the standpoint of godliness; he wants to please God in all he does. He is aware also of his indwelling sinfulness with which he daily battles. He confesses with shame his sinful failures and he grieves because he not only does what he should not do, but he does not do what he should. But this healthy awareness of sin, and this constant repentance can become unbalanced. He can so see the enormity of sin in the sight of a holy God that he loses sight of God's pardon. Sin is indeed ugly, and grief of spirit is appropriate, but spiritual depression is something very different, for it emerges not from a realisation of failure, but from a failure to appreciate the completeness of God's forgiveness.

Of course there is a depression which is directly due to unconfessed sin. It is powerfully expressed in Psalm 32. David had sinned grievously and his adultery with Bathsheba had been covered up, but God had seen it and David's conscience was not at ease. He recalls the misery of it all. "When I kept silence, my bones waxed old through my roaring all the day long. For day and night thy hand was heavy upon me: my moisture is turned into the drought of summer" (Ps. 32: 3-4). But this condition is one for which there is an obvious answer. "I acknowledged my sin unto thee and mine iniquity have I not hid. I said, I will confess my transgressions unto the Lord; and thou forgavest the iniquity of my sin." No wonder he reaches a totally different conclusion from his earlier depressed state. "Be glad in the Lord, and rejoice ye righteous: and shout for joy, all ye that are upright in heart" (v. 11). So we may conclude that there is clearly a necessity for the troubled Christian to come honestly before God with the prayer of another Psalm. "Search me, O God, and know my heart: try me, and know my thoughts: and see if there be any wicked way in me" (Ps. 139: 23-24). God will answer such a prayer by searching us thoroughly, and when He forgives the pardon will be total.

Again and again we have reverted to one continuing element in all the circumstances we have discussed, namely, the unremitting attention of Satan. But he is particularly active in this area of repentance. If he fails to hold us in the path of disobedience, and tastes the bitterness of seeing a Christian in tears of repentance before the Lord, then he will try another ploy. He will attempt to accentuate the sin in such a way as to cast doubt on the forgiveness of God – and this doubt, as we have seen, we must resist. But it is important to recognise that it is not only a doubt which arises from our weakness of faith, but which also emerges from the infiltration of the Evil One into our thinking.

But he can intensify our depression by pressing us even further. To see our sinful failure and to dwell on it even after we have sought God's pardon is to be wide open to the devil's further challenge. He will recall not only recent failures, but failures from a more distant past. His question can beat in with depressing insistence: "Can you call yourself a Christian in view of what you have said and done?" To yield to his accusations is to end in a trough of depression, if not to slide towards the brink of despair. The answer to Satan is still, however, what it was when Jesus employed it so powerfully in the wilderness – the Word of God. When he mounts his accusations, we must fling in his face the promises of Christ. Yes I have sinned, "But if we confess our sins He is faithful and just to forgive us our sins and to cleanse us from all unrighteousness."

A further cause for deep gloom is a truth which in fact can be one of the great answers to depression, but if not applied in the right way it can add to the trouble. That truth is the Christian's membership in the body of Christ. By the miracle wrought by the Holy Spirit he has been united to Christ and incorporated into His body. That means he is organically linked with the other members of the body. This can be a potent influence for encouraging him in times of discouragement, in that he has others to whom to turn, others in whom he can confide, and above all, others who will pray for him. But again Satan will be working very hard to twist that truth so that it becomes a blight rather than a blessing. So the awareness of being a member of the body brings with it a sense of responsibility to live worthily of such a position. The depressed believer, however, instead of finding this a stimulus to holiness, and an encouragement, finds himself even lower in spirit because he feels that by his depression he is failing his fellow-believers. He needs to be careful that in fact he is not guilty of a subtle form of pride, like the person who is reluctant to accept help from anyone because he finds it humiliating to accept what he calls "charity". As members of the body of Christ, it is not only our responsibility to give from our strength, but also our privilege to receive in our weakness. We need to see our membership as a source of help in trouble, rather than merely an occasion for self-reproach.

An allied cause of spiritual depression is the believer's feeling that he is failing as a witness. He is Christ's representative to men. He meets with many who are without God and without hope, with those who have plunged deeply into the pleasures of the world and found them empty, with those who are crying out for a satisfying answer. But how can he speak of the joy of the Lord, or the power of the gospel in setting men free, if he himself is unable to rise above his own troubles? Now it is certainly true that a depressed Christian is no advertisement for the gospel. It is indeed sadly true that he is a hindrance not only to his own witness but to that of his church. But if he lets this drive him further down the despairing path he is adding to his failure. If, on the other hand, it arouses him to action and stimulates him to look and pray more insistently for an answer to his condition, then his justifiable sense of failure will cease to be a cumulative ingredient in a worsening state. It will become a God-given incentive to find a biblical solution.

There are further personal consequences of depression which in a sense are so obvious that they might scarcely seem to warrant attention. But it is well to note them, if only by way of reassurance to any deeply depressed reader that the suggested answers are not shallow formulae which ignore the sufferer's plight. He himself certainly knows the outcome. When, for example, he reads Psalm 42 it speaks so pointedly to his condition. Here is a desperate inner pain allied to a deep sense of failure. Here too is the absence of joy which is aggravated by the memory of past delights. The fellowship of past days, and the times of blessing under the preaching of the Word only tend to heighten the present distress, for one marked feature of depression is inner loneliness. Friends try to help, and their advice may be wise, but this loneliness of spirit tends to confine the troubled soul within an area so restricted that he feels desperately, and at times agonisingly, alone. Yet if he is to break out of this dark cell he must listen to the voice of God as the Spirit speaks through the Scripture. To that biblical testimony we must therefore turn.

It is necessary to clear the ground by means of three negatives. In the first place there is no quick answer to the problem. This is the day of instant solutions. The radio commentators pass their immediate judgement on a situation almost before the events have reached their final stage. The advertising industry is geared to the snap slogan and the slick answer. Sadly this mentality has invaded the churches, and it is assumed all too often that there are neat answers to most spiritual issues, and that the answer can be formulated with a simple brevity. I recall seeing a booklet on the A B C of holiness, an approach which, to use the analogy of climbing the Alps, is to prescribe the chair lift to the top in place of the long haul up the mountainside – with this difference, that the chairlift, unlike the A B C booklet, does get us to the top! It is, however, the long haul which Scripture prescribes, and which proves to be the only satisfying answer to the man who hungers and thirsts for righteousness.

Similarly, in the area of depression the quick answer assumes that a few well chosen texts duly quoted should silence all the problems, and lift the depressed Christian to a level of joyous victory. It ignores the fact that a good physician must make an adequate diagnosis before he prescribes the remedy. Indeed, the quick answer can be not only inadequate but disastrous. It either hurts the sufferer more deeply because its glib smoothness mocks the anguish of his spirit, or it provides a temporary relief, which may be an intensely joyful respite, but can lead to a reaction into an even greater gloom than before.

In the second place, it must be firmly stated that there is no standard answer. The tendency to produce such answers is due, as was noted earlier, to the current evangelical tendency to rely on techniques, and to reduce pastoral counselling to formulae which can be learned by the diligent Christian worker. But God does not deal with men and women in the mass. "I have called thee by thy name, thou art mine," this is the divine approach. The genealogies of the Bible are a reminder that the obscure and forgotten people of history were persons with their own individuality in the sight of God. So even the classification of "introvert" as over against "extrovert" must not mislead us into the idea that there is a standard prescription for a uniform condition. There are general features in the condition of depression which are common to very many people, but it still remains true that there is an intensely personal element in each one's suffering, and God deals with us always as persons rather than as statistics in a psychiatric assessment.

The third negative may at first glance seem to be a discouraging one, but it is not really so if it is taken aright. It is the fact that there is no final answer. This must not be taken to mean that there is no answer at all, and that the victim of depression may therefore lapse into hopelessness. Far from it! There *are* answers which will by God's grace lift us from the depths. Indeed if I was not persuaded that there were answers I would not have attempted to write this chapter, for I would have only been adding misery to an already sorry condition by furnishing a diagnosis without giving any remedy. There is a remedy, but it is not final in the sense that once understood and applied it will lead to a permanent immunity. There are types of depression which are rooted in some physical condition, or some period of particular emotional stress or tension. Such, while they may produce a time of great mental distress, may in fact never be repeated. But there are other forms of depression which are more deep seated for they have their roots in the temperament of the people involved. That temperament remains, and so also does the continuing possibility of the re-emergence of the temptation to be depressed. On the other hand, as the believer learns by God's grace to master his temperament, so also, by that same grace, he learns from one victory over depression to move, not to an alternating condition of defeat and victory, but to a pattern of confronting the enemy as it begins to emerge and countering it with the lessons learnt previously. There will, therefore, be no once-for-all immunisation, so that for the rest of his days he will be free from the problem. The problem may, and indeed almost certainly will recur, but the deliverance of the Lord is also constant, and each victory will help us, as the child's hymn puts it, "some other to win".

There are, however, not only negative considerations; there is a positive reaction as well, and this is well illustrated in Psalm 42. Having spoken of his utterly depressed and wretched condition the writer addresses himself, "Why art thou cast down, O my soul, and why art thou disquieted within me?" Here is the kind of detachment which is a prerequisite to hearing God's answer. The Psalmist has learnt a piece of basic psychology, namely that there is such a thing as self-consciousness. We are not only aware of the world around us and of the people we meet; we are aware of ourselves. So we can reflect on ourselves. We are able to stand back from ourselves and to note the kind of temperament we have, and the type of reaction which we are likely to produce in any given situation. We can, as it were, be spectators viewing the working of our own mind and the surge of our own emotions. We can also move beyond the role of spectator to being that of judge, and this is a vital role, for we must constantly assess our actions and the motives behind them.

Now this ability to stand back and scrutinise ourselves is vitally important in dealing with depression, for our first need is to look honestly at our real condition and to deal firmly with ourselves. What makes this attitude of detachment all the more important is that one outcome of depression is self-pity. We feel sorry for ourselves. We feel we need to be helped and comforted. Sympathy we deem to be the chief requirement rather than firm admonition or reproof. In fact we are wrong, for self-pity is utterly sterile. It simply means that we move round in a small circle and become increasingly weakened, so that we are more and more dependent on various props. What we need to do is to stand back from ourselves and administer a firm word of rebuke. Others are unlikely to do it, for they might feel it was an approach lacking in sympathy and, in addition, they do not know the hidden depths of our spirit and so dare not speak like this. But we, in some measure at least, know ourselves. We can be hard with ourselves in a way that we would not be with others. So we begin by taking ourselves to task.

What the Psalmist is really saying to his soul is this: "What right have you to be cast down?" It is a good question. When we are depressed we think a lot about our problems. We oscillate between tantalising memories of the past, and the present gloom which seems to give no hint of any light in the future. As a result we forget all God's past goodness. We ignore His providential care. We pass over the innumerable blessings which His liberality has showered upon us. Yet, instead of licking our wounds, we should be rebuking ourselves for our ingratitude. "Why art thou cast down O my soul?" With such a gracious God, with such a merciful Saviour, with such a glorious gospel, and with all the blessings which accompany that gospel what an absurd thing it is – worse still, what an ungrateful thing it is – to be so cast down! So we begin to enumerate our blessings. Instead of brooding on our problems and our fears we deliberately set ourselves to reflect on the mercies of God. "Thou shalt remember all the way the Lord thy God hath led thee"; the advice of Deuteronomy 8: 2 still applies. As we remember that God's mercies are new every morning and his faithfulness is great (La. 3: 23) we begin to stand back and see how wrong it is to become so obsessed with our own anxieties and cares that we lose sight of the glorious generosity of our God.

The next step is also seen in Psalm 42. Having questioned himself in terms of a firm rebuke, he then gives himself an equally firm command: "Hope thou in God". The depressed believer has been taken up with himself. That is his problem. The past has not helped him for it has only reminded him, either of his failures or of pleasures no longer with him. The present, with its misery, alone is his, and the future is bleak. No, says the Psalmist, the future is as bright as the faithfulness of God. The unchanging God is the eternally present one who binds the past, the present and the future, into one eternal "now". So the future is not some continued tangle of perplexing uncertainties. It is not merely the prolongation of the present dark tunnel. The future is in God's hands. The God of yesterday is the God of tomorrow, so "hope thou in God".

It is important to notice how this is presented in terms of a personal relationship. It is not some piece of wishful thinking in which we hope that things will turn out more favourably and we shall emerge from this present cloud. Nor is it even simply a prayer for deliverance. It is an attitude of confidence which faces the future and finds its point of reliance in God Himself. I listen to His promises. I hear the note of assurance. But hope reaches beyond the promises to the promiser Himself. I stay myself on Him. I hope in God.

This means a deliberate, and a continuing attitude. I will be tempted to look at my own weakness. I will move from that to the problems. I will go to and fro until I am in the depths of misery, unless, that is, I deliberately turn my thoughts God-wards and set my mind upon Him. The same idea is found in Hebrews 12:1-2. We are called to run the race with all its difficulties, and with our own tendency to tire and give up. But we must run with persistence. How can we do that? By looking at Jesus! The Greek word means literally "looking away". We must turn away from the issues which have so clouded our minds, and set our thoughts firmly on the God who reigns in glory, and in the sympathetic High Priest at His right hand.

"I shall yet praise Him," says the Psalmist, "for the help of His countenance." How much may be conveyed by the expression on a person's face. A smile of welcome, a frown of disapproval, a pained look or an encouraging one, all these are conveyed by a quick glance. In the close-knit familiarity of a family we are even more likely to detect another's reaction in his facial expression. So the Psalmist speaks of looking into the face of God, and seeing there the encouragement and the stimulus to lift up his heart afresh.

Now it is easy to see how this applies in a human situation where we can actually, and in a physical sense, see the expression on a friend's face. But in what sense, and in what way, do I see the face of God? Clearly it is with the eye of faith that I must look, but to what do I look? When the Bible uses human terms to speak of God it intends to convey to us the ideas which are implicit in those terms. So when it speaks of the right arm of the Lord it refers to His strength, and when it speaks of the eyes of the Lord it refers to His omniscience. So when it here speaks of His face it refers to God as He makes Himself known. To look into His face is to turn by faith to the revelation He has given us in His word, and to see Him as He is made known in all the facets of His being.

This means that the more deeply we press into the biblical truths concerning God, the more readily we shall be able to turn to them and reflect on them in time of stress. So, too, if we are content to sit week after week under a liberal ministry rather than one which expounds the whole counsel of God, we need not be surprised if in the testing day we have such an inadequate grasp of God's glorious being that the going is extremely hard. "Thy Word have I hid in my heart that I might not sin against thee" (Ps. 119: 11). This is not only a reminder of an essential element in a life of holiness, it also applies in this area of depression. A mind well stored with the truths of God's Word will be well furnished to resist the attacks of the evil one, and also to rouse us from our depression to renewed hope.

But this look into God's face is not an act which immediately solves the problem. We are not back in the area of the glib answer and the standard formula for a quick solution of our problem. It can be a real battle of faith, not only to look into God's face, but to keep looking. This again comes out clearly in Psalm 42. It would seem as if the Psalmist has emerged from the cloud of depression into the sunshine of renewed fellowship with God. He is indeed praising the Lord for His help. Then suddenly he seems to be back where he was before. The burst of praise suddenly gives way to the pathetic admission: "O my God, my soul is cast down within me." Here is a reaction which often comes in the battle with depression. There is a moment when the truth dawns and the light penetrates the darkness. Then, suddenly, the old fears flood in, the waves of depression sweep uncontrollably over the spirit and one is again in the depths.

Nevertheless it is to be noted that the psalmist does not go right back. It is not a case of a complete reversal of the gains already made. The lesson learnt is still applied, though clearly it is a struggle to apply it. With all the renewed gloom of spirit, he still recalls the answer he has just learnt. So he continues, "Therefore will I remember thee". We must continue to look into the Father's face; we must continue to look away to the end of the race where the pioneer and perfecter of faith awaits the victorious runner. There may be set-backs and as a result we may feel we are not gaining ground. But in fact we are making progress, as each fresh assault of Satan and each fresh wave of doubt or fear or anxiety are countered in the way the psalmist shows us here. So we will turn from our gloom to reflect on the loving kindness of the Lord. We will deliberately recall also that because "He that keepeth Israel shall neither slumber nor sleep" we will find Him as near in the lonely sleepless hours of the night as in the friendly context of a family afternoon gathering. So the psalmist can sing, "In the night His song shall be with me, and my prayer unto the God of my life."

As he persists in his attitude of faith, and as he gets his attention off his difficulties and turns from the gloom which envelops him to the God who is still with him, a change is detected in the psalmist himself. Again, he turns to God. But where he has formerly looked into the face of God and found encouragement, now we can see a change in his own face. He moves from "I shall yet praise Him for the help of His countenance" to an even more confident "I will yet praise Him, who is the health of my countenance and my God." One can sense the change. The deeply depressed man with his inner gloom showing in his face has become the forward-looking believer whose very expression reflects his new awareness of the peace of God which passes all understanding.

The apostle Paul summarises so many of the themes of this chapter in one brief but glorious statement, which has been a stabilising word to many a discouraged and depressed Christian. "In nothing be anxious but in everything by prayer and supplication with thanksgiving let your requests be made known unto God, and the peace of God which passes all understanding shall keep your hearts and minds in Christ Jesus" (Ph. 4: 6-7). Here is the firm resolve to resist the anxiety which depresses. Here is the earnest prayer which looks steadily to the God of all grace. Here too is the thanksgiving which recounts God's past mercies and takes fresh heart from the recital. Here finally is the peace of God guarding the soul. Paul was writing to Christians in Philippi, a garrison town near the frontier of the empire. Along the walls the legionaries stood on guard so that the citizens could sleep in security. So too the peace of God stands guard over the soul. The devil will continue to mount his attacks. The traitor within – the old sinful nature – will be tempted to open the gates. But resistance will be mounted and, in face of the doubts and anxieties and depressions which are part of Satan's armoury, the peace of God mounts a firm guard. So the call comes insistently, "Lift up your hearts", to which the appropriate reply of faith is "We lift them up unto the Lord." It is in that reply, not used as an easy formula, but viewed as a continuing attitude that the ultimate conquest of depression is to be found.

CHAPTER 13

WALKING IN THE DARK

The title of this chapter comes from a verse in Isaiah chapter 50:
"Who is among you that feareth the Lord, that obeyeth the voice
of his servant, that walketh in darkness, and hath no light? Let him
trust in the name of the Lord, and stay upon his God" (Is. 50: 10).
In a famous sermon preached on this text in the last century J. C.
Philpot used as a title the telling description: "The heir of heaven
walking in the dark". It is an apt summary of the theme of this
verse – and indeed the theme of this present book – that there is an
experience of darkness of spirit which can affect the Christian. A
closer study of this word from Isaiah is appropriate, not only to
summarise much of what has been said in earlier chapters, but also
by way of re-emphasising that there are answers from God for such
a condition.

To many Christians, the idea that a believer could face a protracted
period of darkness is foreign to their thinking. Brought up in the
context of an evangelicalism which has instant answers for so many
problems, they find it hard to conceive the kind of condition which
the prophet describes. They have listened to the testimonies which
speak of joy and victory, but seldom seem to touch on the darker
sides of spirituality. They have sung the current songs and choruses
which tend to stress the delights and pleasures of being a Christian,
without hinting at the shadows which may cloud the sky. They have
been reared on teaching which is so concerned to hand out assurance
that it dismisses doubts and fears as reactions not to be considered
seriously.

The result of all this is that if they do go through a time of darkness
of soul they are inclined to use the lash of conscience to whip them-

selves unmercifully. They search frantically for some act of blatant disobedience which has caused their trouble. Or they go to the other extreme and use the cheerful company and easy praise of their friends as a way of escape from their problems.

Yet here is a condition which can be quite protracted. The term "walk" is used in Scripture to describe a continuing condition. So this is not the fleeting cloud which covers the sun for a brief moment and brings with it a slight chill. It is the darkness of an overcast sky which shows no sign of a break. It is a condition which, as we have seen earlier, can be an accompaniment of depression or bereavement. It can also be due to a particular assault of the devil on our assurance of salvation. It may be due to a deep dissatisfaction with a low level of spiritual experience, coupled with a radical questioning of all that we believe. While the condition may well be accentuated by the kind of temperament we have, it is not confined to one type of Christian. The most thoroughgoing extrovert, who takes his Christian living as seriously as Scripture intends we should, may have as deep an experience of darkness of soul as his most introspective friend.

It is important to notice that Isaiah is not discussing a condition where those affected have made an empty and rather formal profession. Nor is he describing believers who have become slack and undisciplined in their living. This is not a picture of the backslider. Indeed the latter – such is the tragedy of his situation – may be walking cheerfully in the light, even though it is a false dawn. Those however who are in view here, are not only true believers, but are also deeply concerned with godly living.

In the first place, they are those who "fear the Lord". The word "fear" in the Old Testament is closely allied to the word "trust" in the New. It does not signify the troubles of an aroused conscience, nor the dread of coming judgement. It speaks rather of a spirit of deep reverence. The man who fears the Lord has a profound sense of awe before his Creator. He has come to grasp, even if in a limited way, the majesty and transcendent power of the God who rules over all. He has, as a result, a serious approach to the things of God. He has no time for spiritual trifling, for such a shallow approach is an affront to God most holy.

But the fear of the Lord also means a spirit of reliance upon God. It involves a recognition of God's gracious activities. He is the Redeemer who saves His people from their sins. He is the Good

Shepherd who guides them. He is the Father who cares for them. So to fear God is to rely on His promises and, indeed, to reach beyond the promises to the One who makes them, and to trust personally and directly in Him.

Such fear brings an attitude of obedience. A reverent approach to God means a humble awareness of His sovereign right to declare to His people how they shall live and behave. In such an approach there is no place for the qualified obedience which tries to reserve areas of life for personal control, or which attempts to set limits to the requirements of God. The fear of the Lord means a loving desire to please Him in all things. It implies a deep concern lest by carelessness or selfishness God should be grieved. To fear is to obey Him, not with the dragging feet of a reluctant conscript, but with the glad response of a lover.

Furthermore, these God-fearing believers obey God's servant. The question at once arises: "Who is this servant?" The answer seems to be quite plain, for this section of the prophecy has a great deal to say about the suffering servant of Jehovah. It is, in fact, a prophetic portrait of the coming Saviour, the Lord Jesus Christ, whose passion is so graphically portrayed in the fifty-third chapter of Isaiah's prophecy.

These believers know the Saviour, for they obey "His voice". To hear His voice implies a personal knowledge of the One who speaks. So Jesus spoke of His flock: "The sheep follow Him for they know His voice." A voice has differing tones and carries particular meanings to close friends in its very cadence. So, to hear the Saviour's voice is to be alert and intent to detect all that He has to say. Once again we return to the kind of people being described. They are those who study the Word, take a delight in the preaching of the Word, and have a deep concern to press on in holiness of life.

It has been necessary to stress the essential godliness of those who are here described as walking in the dark, in order to eliminate the notion that such a state is inevitably a mark of spiritual decline. There is indeed the darkness of an unregenerate condition. So Paul reminds the Ephesians, "Ye were sometime darkness, but now are ye light in the Lord" (Ep. 5: 8). He urges them to repudiate "the unfruitful works of darkness" (Ep. 5: 11). John, in a similar vein, speaks of the ungodly as those who walk in darkness (1 Jn. 1: 6). But this kind of darkness is totally different from the situation of the true believer who "walks in the dark and has no light".

There is a vast difference between a deep cave or a mine shaft where the sunshine has never penetrated, and a dark country road at night. Superficially they are alike in that there is a common condition of darkness, but in fact they stand in marked contrast, for the darkness of the road is purely temporary. It came with sunset and it will be dispersed by the coming dawn. So the darkness of the unbeliever is one of unrelieved gloom, and if the light of the gospel does not shine into his heart he will end in the darkness of an endless night. But the darkness of spirit which the believer may experience is but a prelude to a dawn of renewed blessing and, ultimately, to the glorious sunrise of heaven.

The marks of this condition are summed up in the statement "they have no light". It is in marked contrast with the confident affirmation of Psalm 119: 105, "Thy word is a lamp unto my feet and a light unto my path". Yet it is a situation by no means uncommon. The Christian ceases to find any help from his Bible reading. It is as if the Word has gone dead for him, and though he continues dutifully to read the Scriptures each day, there is little life in them for him. The very texts which in the past filled him with joyful assurance now seem so much printer's ink in an oft-read book. No wonder he feels that he is stumbling uncertainly where formerly he stepped out with confidence.

The landmarks have also disappeared. To walk in the countryside on a really dark night is to be blind to the beauty of the surrounding landscape. The familiar hill, the well known clumps of trees, the neatly-trimmed garden hedge, all are lost to view. He can look neither back along the road he has already walked, nor forward to the one he has still to cover. A similar obscuring of the spiritual landmarks can affect the Christian. He looks back but he no longer is able to recall with confident assurance the early days of his Christian life. Indeed he may be so beset by doubts that he may even ask whether he is on the right road at all. So the heavenly goal also recedes from view and the signposts of the Word directing him to the celestial city are lost in the gloom.

Worst of all he loses sight of his guide. The twenty-third Psalm had so often stirred his soul as he caught a glimpse of the Shepherd leading him even in the dark valley. The Lord Jesus had, in the past, spoken to his soul in His gracious promise: "When He putteth forth His own sheep He goeth before them". But now the Lord has become no more than an idea in his mind to which he clings rather

114

desperately; yet somehow there seems to be no warm response in his heart. He believes in the Lord Jesus Christ, or so he claims, but there is a nagging doubt, for in the darkness he seems to have lost sight of the Saviour. Job's distress of mind is much more akin to his present mood: "I go forward, but He is not there; and backward, but I cannot perceive Him: on the left hand, where He doth work, but I cannot behold Him: He hideth Himself on the right hand, that I cannot see Him" (Jb. 23: 8-9).

But despair has no place in the vocabulary of the Christian, nor indeed has a numbed acquiescence in his condition. God speaks to him in the darkness and it is a word of encouragement and hope. It is not simply a call to wait hopefully for things to alter. It is rather a call to action. He is to do certain things. He is to adopt certain attitudes. There is nothing vague in the spirituality of Scripture. We are not left like Mr. Micawber waiting for something to turn up to change our situation. We may be walking in the dark but God remains the same and faith therefore must be exercised.

The first insistent call to the believer directs him afresh to God Himself: "Let him trust in the name of the Lord." When the Bible uses the phrase "the name of the Lord" it speaks of God as He has revealed Himself. He dwells in light unapproachable as far as human wisdom is concerned. He is the high and lofty one dwelling in heights no human power can scale. But He has revealed Himself. He is not a God dwelling in some remote silence so that we can do no more than speculate. He has made Himself known.

He has made Himself known as our Father caring for us, guiding us, protecting us. But His care remains the same even in the darkness. A child may not be able to see his father as they walk along the dark road but he hears his voice and feels his hand. Indeed he may be far more aware of his father's nearness in the dark than when he scampers ahead on a sunny afternoon. So the Christian needs to remind himself that his Father is still with him and, although he cannot see the Lord, the Lord can still see him.

Then again the Lord has revealed Himself as the Saviour. The present darkness may seem dense to the believer, but he remembers another darkness which was impenetrable to human eyes, in which God's own Son died at Golgotha. So his present darkness is but a passing shadow, and beyond it he must set his mind and heart upon the Saviour who loved him and died for him and who still prays for him in heaven.

The name of the Lord speaks also of God's revelation of Himself in the person of the Holy Spirit. "I will not leave you orphans," said Jesus as He promised His disciples the gift of the Holy Spirit. He has come. He dwells within us. He will not forsake us. An orphan condition is incompatible with His continuing ministry. So we must not succumb to the doubts and fears which surround us in the darkness. We must turn afresh to the realisation of faith, that the Spirit of God has actually made our bodies His temple.

Then comes the further word of God through the prophet: "Let him trust in the name of the Lord and stay upon his God." Let him rely upon his God; let him find a solid ground for his confidence in his God. The personal pronoun is important. The God on whom he is to rely is "*his* God", for He is the God of the covenant.

A covenant is a relationship in which promises are made and pledges are given. It is a fitting word to describe the link between God and His people. Of course it differs from all human covenants in that, in this one, God has taken the initiative. God has made the promises and given the pledges; it is "the covenant of grace". It brings guilty sinners from a state of rebellion into a union with God Almighty in which He pledges Himself to be their God. "You shall be my people," He says with gracious forgiveness. The reply of faith is glad thanksgiving: "Thou art our God."

But to speak of a covenant is to speak of something which cannot be broken or annulled. True, men may break their covenants; the unending list of broken treaties is a standing witness to human unfaithfulness. But God is faithful and He does not go back on His promises. Indeed He has backed His promises with His own character. He has pledged Himself to us and it is unthinkable that God would break His solemn pledge and so betray His own honour. The covenant is therefore as sure in the darkest night as in the brightest day. It is not affected by the passage of time nor by adverse circumstances. So we may stay ourselves upon our God.

This God of the covenant is the everlasting God. He is no broken reed. He is not a cistern which fails. He is not a faulty foundation which is a prelude to ruin. He is the everlasting rock of ages. We may be beset by fears about the future, or by doubts which darken the sky. Let us stay ourselves upon our God. Let us realise that He is "from everlasting to everlasting". How great and glorious He is and by contrast how little our problems become when set alongside His unchanging power.

116

God, through Isaiah, puts it to us as a question: "Who is among you that feareth the Lord . . . that walketh in darkness and hath no light?" It is as if He would reach into the fellowship with a sympathetic concern to find those who are particularly troubled. He does not deal with His people in the mass. He knows that there are those who are under peculiar stress and facing acute tensions, and He singles them out for special concern. It is as though He addresses them directly and personally. Are you walking in darkness? Does the light seem to have failed as far as you are concerned? Remember that the God of the covenant is your God. He is unchanging in His love and mercy and faithfulness. So trust in His name and stay yourself upon your God. In that confidence you will find peace. The darkness will give way to the brightness of the glory of the Lord.

CHAPTER 14

BIBLICAL CASE HISTORY (3)

JEREMIAH

Called by God to prophesy to a nation which resented his message, Jeremiah faced a long ministry in which misunderstanding and loneliness, misrepresentation and disappointment, were continuing features. At the outset he had shrunk from the task, pleading his youth and inexperience. He had only gone forward under the pressure of God's voice. Longing at times to escape from the burden he only kept going because of that same compelling Word of the Lord. Called in a tragic hour for his people, he lived to see the tragedy reach its dark conclusion; yet because of his own passionate involvement he could never remain an aloof commentator. Indeed it is one of the outstanding characteristics of his prophecy, that the man and the message are inextricably bound together. The vehemence of the denunciations of sin, the urgency of the warnings of judgement, and the gracious words of mercy, all come with an intensity born in his own struggles in his own soul. Yet, with all his spiritual greatness – and he is one of the truly great men of Scripture – he was still very human. So it is as a man, in all the loneliness of suffering, that he still speaks to us. To those discouraged by adversity, to those for whom depression at times hovers on the cliff edge of despair, to those who know deep loneliness of spirit, Jeremiah speaks, not only through his prophetic message, but also through his own experiences.

He faced the utter frustration of diagnosing the real plight of the nation while people generally rejected his words. There was an abundance of popular preachers who, as such men usually do, gave a superficial estimate of the situation and prescribed an equally facile solution. We can sense the bitterness in Jeremiah's description of these false preachers: "They have healed the hurt of the daughter of my people slightly, saying, Peace, peace; when there is no peace" (8: 11). What made it even worse was that there seemed to be a universal commitment to complacency: "The prophets prophecy falsely, and the priests bear rule by their means; and my people love to have it so: and what will ye do in the end thereof?" (5: 31).

To be a disturber of that complacency was no popular role. It is no wonder that the opposition raged so fiercely. Nor was it only a negative reaction from the general run of people; it came also in his own native Anathoth and even from members of his own family (11: 21, 12: 6). Like the Messiah to whom he looked as the messenger of the new covenant, Jeremiah had to learn that "a prophet is not without honour, save in his own country, and in his own house" (Mt. 13: 57). To be deeply misunderstood, when in fact your whole aim is to help those who misjudge your motives, is always an added pain.

But they did not rest content with misunderstanding. There was the added agony of misrepresentation. He himself loved his country and his nation very deeply. It was this love which caused him such deep pain. One can detect the inner travail in his cry to God: "O that my head were waters, and mine eyes a fountain of tears, that I might weep day and night for the slain of the daughter of my people" (9: 1). Yet they could pervert his words in such a grotesque fashion, that they misrepresented him as a hater of his people and a traitor.

Inevitably he was a lonely figure. Where many a preacher has found in his wife a source of strength in difficult days, Jeremiah was denied that comfort. Where others have been able to relax in the context of family life, he faced a solitary path. "The word of the Lord came also unto me, saying, Thou shalt not take thee a wife, neither shalt thou have sons or daughters in this place" (16: 1-2). In this unusual calling he was to signal, in his own deprivation, the tragic dislocation and destruction of family life which would come with national judgement. The signal was faithfully given, but at tremendous cost to the lonely prophet. It is no wonder that he has been seen as one of the clearest foreshadowings in the Old Testament of the suffering, lonely, and rejected Saviour.

But the conflict was not only with the unending opposition, and with the terrible circumstances in which he lived and ministered. The battle was also fought in his own soul. Perhaps more than any other book in Scripture, apart from the Psalms, this prophecy lays bare a man's soul. We are allowed to enter the sanctuary which is the inviolate area of the human spirit, and to listen to a man in the deepest agony remonstrating with God, pleading to be relieved of his burden, crying in the darkness until the sob finds no echo and he falls silent. Yet it is in these inner struggles that he is such a potent minister to the troubled heart. Here is no easy purveyor of religious theories. Here is one of the great sufferers of Scripture sharing with us in our own grief and loneliness.

One of his earliest complaints to God comes in chapter twelve. It is not one that is peculiar to Jeremiah, for we hear it again and again in the Psalms. It is the problem of reconciling the righteousness of God with His apparent tolerance of ungodliness and blatant injustice. "Righteous art thou, O Lord, when I plead with thee: yet let me talk with thee of thy judgements: wherefore doth the way of the wicked prosper? wherefore are all they happy that deal very treacherously?" (12: 1). Why should the faithful minister battle on in face of apathy and opposition, while the glib-tongued practitioners of an easy religious profession receive popular esteem? Why should the godly widow face poverty, or the honest workman a crippling injury, while exploiters batten on the misery of the weak, and continue to flourish?

For Jeremiah the question has undertones of a more personal complaint, for he himself is the sufferer, and it is his message which is being treated with scorn and contempt. It is not surprising therefore that God's answer to the question is not a theoretical one, but has a direct personal application. It comes as a challenging question in which there is a firm word of rebuke: "If you have raced with men on foot, and they have wearied you, how will you compete with horses? And if in a safe land you fall down, how will you do in the jungle of the Jordan?" (12: 5 R.S.V.). There will be greater testings ahead, and more complex trials. If he falters in face of these initial obstacles, how will he fare when the going becomes really rough?

What he, and we, need to learn is that God has not abdicted His throne. He is still the sovereign Lord God Almighty. He may not disclose His secrets to us but we may rest assured that He will perfectly work out His purposes. This means that the testings are not due to a mere flowing together of adverse circumstances, nor are they due to the astute schemes of ungodly men. God is still working out "all things after the counsel of His own will" (Ep. 1: 11) and part of this outworking is the testing of the faith of His people.

There is a further lesson here. God's tests are graded to suit each stage of our spiritual progress. A skilful teacher does not insult the intelligence of his most able pupils by giving them problems whose solution is obvious. But on the other hand he does not load the beginners with a test so difficult that they lose heart. A good teacher aims to stretch the mind of his pupils in proportion to their ability and progress. So too God, the great instructor, neither makes things too easy nor permits them to become intolerably difficult. "There hath no temptation taken you but such as is common to man: but God is faithful, who will not suffer you to be tempted above that ye are able; but will with the temptation also make a way to escape, that ye may be able to bear it" (1 Co. 10: 13).

There will always be further tests in the future and some of them may be of great severity. But the battle of the future must not be waged today. What Jeremiah had to learn was that he must face his present situation and learn to deal with that. Failure now would mean a weakening of his ability to cope with greater problems ahead. Victory now would not only encourage him, but also strengthen his spiritual fibre for the trials still to come. We are not to try to anticipate the future. Yet awareness of the reality of the continuing struggle will impel us all the more urgently to fight the good fight of faith now. The present, after all, is simply one phase of the battle, and in learning to prove God now, we are preparing, in the best way possible, for the greater onslaughts ahead.

The next record of his inner struggle comes in chapter 15. Like water suddenly surging through a burst dam, he is so overwhelmed with the hatred he faces that the words tumble out in utter agony. Like many another, he wishes he had never been born. "Woe is me, my mother, that thou hast borne me a man of strife and a man of contention to the whole earth! I have neither lent on usury, nor men have lent to me on usury; yet every one of them doth curse me" (15: 10). One hears an echo of the Lord Jesus Christ Himself: "They hated me without a cause."

But having begun, the bitter stream of words pours on, and that in spite of God's reassurance that God, not man, is in control, and He will vindicate His servant in due time. It is no answer in Jeremiah's mood of bitterness. Has he not been faithful to the Lord? He has gladly received the words of God (1: 16) making them his own, and taking his delight in them. Yet the result is continual pain. So the complaint rages on until Jeremiah oversteps the bounds which the fear of God should have placed on his lips. In one grim moment the festering resentment against God breaks the surface as he accuses the Lord of having deceived him. God has called him and he has responded. Yet look at the catalogue of misery his obedience has produced. So he cries in bitterness of heart, "Why is my pain perpetual, and my wound incurable, which refuseth to be healed? Wilt thou be altogether unto me as a liar, and as waters that fail?" (15: 18).

To speak of God as a deceiver and a broken cistern was appalling. Yet if we are honest with ourselves, will we not admit that the thought which lies behind the words, a thought prompted by Satan, has not only come unbidden to the mind but has not always been rejected as it ought to be? Certainly God views such a reaction very seriously. There is no word of further encouragement, but one of stern rebuke. Such a complaining slander against God calls for immediate repentance. He is reminded that a commission from God does not confer an immunity from sinful failure. So says God, "If you utter what is precious and not what is worthless" – as he had been doing – "and if you return in repentance the Lord will restore you and renew your commission to serve Him" (15: 19 R.S.V.).

The lesson is plain. No amount of pain can ever justify our impugning the integrity of God – "Let God be true but every man a liar." Satan will deceive us, and we may deceive one another, but God will never deceive. In our moments of near despair we may lurch towards that awful moment of slandering God. At such a time we need to recall the source of these terrible thoughts. They come from the liar who deceived Eve in the garden of Eden, as he misrepresented the Lord to her. His lies must be rejected. We must repent of our own unworthy thoughts, even if they have not broken the surface as they did with the prophet. The reply of God to his repentance is His constant answer to His penitent servants. It is renewed assurance of God's grace to face the opposition: "They shall fight against thee, but they shall not prevail against thee: for I am with thee, to save thee and to deliver thee, saith the Lord" (15: 20).

There is one further bout of complaints and with them the darkest experience of all. Again it is the pressure of the unceasing contempt which he faces; he has been put in the stocks as a public spectacle. He forgets the awful failure of the past when he gave way to the devil's slanders. He forgets the rebuke he then received for speaking what was vile. So he returns in the bitterness of his complaint to the same charge, "O Lord thou hast deceived me, and I am deceived: thou art stronger than I and hast prevailed" (20: 7). It is his protest against the superior strength of the Lord which had overwhelmed his earliest resistance to the divine call, and had continued to compel him to preach to a rebellious people. Yet the outcome was only wretchedness for himself, with no compensating sign of repentance from the people. He had wanted to give up preaching – how many a discouraged preacher will sympathise with his feelings – but he cannot. How can a man whom God has entrusted with His Word give up? Jeremiah certainly could not do so. "Then I said, I will not make mention of Him, nor speak any more in His name. But His Word was in mine heart as a burning fire shut up in my bones, and I was weary with forbearing, and I could not stay" (20: 9). One hears an echo in the reply of the rugged prophet of Tekoa, when the worldly ecclesiastic tried to silence him. "I was no prophet," says Amos, "nor was I a prophet's son; but I was a herdsman, and a gatherer of sycamore fruit; and the Lord took as I followed the flock, and the Lord said unto me, go, prophesy unto my people Israel" (Am. 7: 14-15).

Jeremiah gets a grip upon himself and reassures himself (20: 11) with the reminder that the Lord is with him so that his foes will stumble. So he commits his cause afresh to God (v. 12) and indeed rejoices in God's deliverance (v. 13). But such is the see-saw of a time like this, of great mental and spiritual turmoil, that he reverts from these moments of confidence to a further time of deep depression. Yet in that very reaction we can find comfort, as we learn that the way out of deep discouragement is not one quick step into the sunlight, but is at times hesitant and stumbling. What a sudden drop there is from the heights of joy to the depths of misery in Jeremiah's words: "Sing unto the Lord, praise ye the Lord; for he hath delivered the soul of the poor from the hand of evildoers. Cursed be the day wherein I was born: let not the day wherein my mother bore me be blessed" (20: 13-14). It is the same sudden reversal of mood which we saw in Psalm 42. From the confident words "I shall yet praise Him for the help of His countenance", there is the drastic change to the cry "O my God my soul is cast down within me". It is the kind of sudden change which is all too familiar to anyone who has tasted this sort of dark discouragement. But in sensing an affinity with the stricken spirit of Jeremiah we can also draw comfort from his God. That comfort does not come at once. This time there is no reassuring word, nor does Jeremiah say anything which gives any hint of renewed peace of mind. The chapter ends in utter darkness of soul. It is a similar experience to that described in Psalm 88 which ends not in the dawn of renewed hope but in the darkness of an unrelieved wretchedness. There are such times in the experience of the Christian, when darkness seems to hang over the soul. There is no easy answer. The texts do not come. He feels utterly alone. Yet even in that dark hour he learns lessons which he would not have learned elsewhere. He learns to cry to God with a new earnestness. He realises in a fresh way the sinfulness of his own heart. He appreciates with a deeper wonder what it means to be saved from eternal darkness, compared to which his present experience is like a passing shadow. He finds his thoughts turning from the things of this world, which have no answer in such an hour of need, to the heavenly world where the joy of the Lord will be an unending experience.

Obviously Jeremiah did not remain in this condition of spiritual desolation. He emerged to renewed hope and to a continuing ministry. From the lessons learned he was not only to continue his ministry of warning, but was able to write the great passages in his prophecy (chapter 30-33) which have been given the title of "the book of consolation". Clearly he had learnt in the darkness to rely on the unchanging faithfulness of his God.

Our darkness may be as intense as Jeremiah's, when the landmarks have disappeared and we lose sight both of past providences and of future goals. Our awareness of the presence of the Lord may have gone. Yet even then we discover the truth of Francis Thompson's words:

> "Is my gloom after all,
> Shade of His hand, outstretched caressingly?"

We may not see Him in the darkness but, thank God, He continues to see us. We may, in our distress of soul, forget His promises to us, but mercifully He does not forget them. We can echo the Psalmist as he worships the Lord: "The darkness and the night are both alike to thee". In that assurance, even in the deepest darkness, we may stay ourselves upon God.

CHAPTER 15

TO SUM UP

The apostle Paul is master both of the sustained argument and the pithy statement. In his epistle to the Romans the argument is developed with great power as assertions are made and demonstrated, objections are faced and conclusions drawn prior to pointed application. But again and again there are the brief statements which in a few terse words sum up so much of the argument, and by their succinct character impress the truth deeply in the mind. The added bonus is that their lucid brevity rivets them in the memory, to be recalled, as circumstances demand, for fresh consideration and timely application. One such verse, and one which aptly summarises so much of the argument of this present book, is Romans 12: 12: "Rejoicing in hope, patient in tribulation, continuing instant in prayer".

One can easily see that the central phrase of the three—"patient in tribulation" is, as it were, supported by the other two. The recurring question for the sufferer is clearly: "How may I persevere in face of affliction? Even when I have learned many of the lessons which God is teaching me, how do I work it out in the actual everyday struggle of coping with my own pain, or of endeavouring to care for others in their trials?" The answer is summarised here in Paul's two supporting phrases. You are to persevere in face of suffering, and in order to do this you must learn on the one side to rejoice in hope, and on the other to continue persistently in prayer.

Turning to the first of the auxiliary phrases – "rejoicing in hope" – we need to remind ourselves at the outset that hope here is used in its distinctively Christian sense. Paul uses the definite article – it is literally "the hope". This may be viewed as the special hope which is implicit in the gospel, or it may be taken in the more personal sense of "your hope". Both shades of meaning are not only possible, but in fact complement one another. It is indeed the hope given by the gospel which is in view, but it is given only to those who by faith have embraced the gospel. So it is not some vaguely optimistic notion that all will turn out well in the long run. It is rather the conviction enjoyed by those who through the gospel have come to know the living God, that this same eternal God will work out His purposes. Furthermore, hope is persuaded that the outworking of these purposes means mercy and love for the sufferer, and glory for the God of all comfort and consolation.

Hope reaches into the unknown future and finds that, although the details of that future are a closed book, the God of the future is the God both of the past and of the present. Indeed it is only our human way of thinking and speaking which refers to God in this way, as if He were part of the process of changing time like ourselves. We can speak of what we were doing yesterday, what we are doing today, and what we aim to do tomorrow. We have our past, our present and our future. We are creatures of time, living by the watch, by the diary, by the calendar, but when God speaks He uses His self-revealing title: "I am". He is always in the present tense. He is the great unchanging one. He is "from everlasting to everlasting" (Ps. 90: 2). "With Him there is no variableness, neither shadow cast by turning" (Ja. 1: 17). He is the eternal God. So my future is His present. What to me is still unknown is to Him like an open book. Hope then faces the future not with a shrug of fatalistic despair, nor with a tentative piece of wishful thinking but with assurance. God is. That is the foundation of our confidence. It is the ground of our hope.

In my native County Down the roads are often hilly because of the underlying boulder clay – or so I learnt in elementary geology at school. In practice I learned it the hard way when cycling to school in days when the government did not provide free transport. There was always another hill ahead. If, on cycling further afield one found a new stretch of road then one's vision was limited to the top of the next hill, and for a cyclist that is a very circumscribed horizon. But more recently I have often flown over that same countryside. From twenty thousand feet you are no longer hemmed in by the hedges on each side of the road, and by the next hill in front. You can sweep across the whole panorama of the countryside from the mountains of Mourne to the Irish Sea. Those hills, up which I used to push, seem mere variations in the pattern of the landscape. Clearly it depends on one's vantage point.

Hope constantly adopts the Christian's vantage point, which is God's view of time and God's survey of history. To look ahead from a purely human standpoint is only to see the next hill – the continuing pain, the persistent sorrow, the debilitating illness with its relentless progress, the grief of seeing a loved one decline further either physically or mentally. All we can do, if that is the limit of our horizon, is to stumble on as best we can. But for the Christian the view from heaven transforms the outlook. The hill of suffering seems all the steeper because it has followed a gentle pleasant slope of easy days; but seen as one element in a great pattern being worked out by one who is almighty and all loving, it becomes part of a landscape where the total scenic effect is superb. In times of intense pain the fog of perplexity may hang so low that I cannot see even the summit of the next hill. But when faith lays hold afresh of the promises of God then hope like a fresh breeze dissipates the fog and I can see, just as God, the ever-present one, sees. It is true – though fool that I am, I doubted it – that the sufferings of this present time are not worthy to be compared with the glory that shall be revealed.

In the roll-call of the heroes of faith in Hebrews 11 the constant theme is this forward look. "These all died in faith, not having received the promises, but having seen them afar off, and were persuaded of them, and embraced them, and confessed that they were strangers and pilgrims on the earth" (He. 11:13). The chapter is a catalogue of suffering. Yet these were men and women who refused to capitulate to the pains and sorrows and persecution of the moment. As citizens of the heavenly city they had their thoughts focused on the triumph ahead. They endured "as seeing Him who is invisible" (v. 27). Their conviction as to the consistency and faithfulness of God led them to a steady confidence in the reliability of His promises, and so to a quiet assurance that He would carry out all that He said He would do. Hope rides high in the heavens, borne up by the gracious promises of the Almighty, and from this lofty vantage point views the passing troubles of the present in their true perspective.

The supreme embodiment of this hope is of course the Lord Jesus Christ Himself. He faced sufferings of a depth and intensity beyond our understanding, and certainly far beyond our experience. Yet He endured not with some stoic passivity, like Socrates enduring approaching death as the victim of Athenian injustice, but with the hope which in turn He shares with His disciples. So, says Hebrews 12: 2, "For the joy that was set before Him He endured the cross, despising the shame, and is set down at the right hand of the throne of God". All that men could see on that grim day outside Jerusalem was the bleeding victim of human injustice. That was all His own disciples could see, as their high hopes crumbled in the midst of the mockery of His tormentors. Their messianic king, whom they had expected to sweep the Roman forces out of the land, died in agony on a Roman scaffold while Roman legionaries threw dice for His clothes. How abject and pathetic it all was. Yet He is shouting out in triumph, "It is finished". Why was He so sure, and why was He able to endure? Surely it was because the joy which was yet in the future was a present reality. In what seemed to be the dying embers of a failed life-work, hope was lighting up the torch of joy. Hope still does the same in our sorrow and in our pain.

Turning then to the other phrase – "continuing instant in prayer" – it must be stressed that it is prayer as it is described in the Bible, and as it has been exercised by the people of God down the years. So it is not the half despairing plea of someone who has really no love for God at all, but tries prayer, as he might term it, as one possible answer to his problems. Such an exercise may afford a man a temporary emotional release but it does not produce the fruit of an abiding peace of soul. Nor is prayer the sporadic intercession which only arises in times of emergency and subsides when the crises are past. Such is all too often what men call prayer, and yet it is largely self-centred and, even if it moves outwards to pray for someone else, has little concern for the glory of God and indeed little awareness of what should be the aim in view in such praying for others.

True prayer is the attitude and the resultant expression of one who has come to know God as Father. This, as Paul expounds in Romans 8, is the outcome of the gracious work of adoption by which God adopts us into His family. Accompanying this is the gift of the Holy Spirit who assures us as to our adoption, and gives us the confidence to pray, "Our Father". Such prayer is not limited to asking, but embraces the whole sweep of adoration, praise, confession, thanksgiving and intercession. While it arises by the Spirit's prompting, it is none the less a spiritual exercise in which we need to mature. To use the title of Andrew Murray's book, we enrol "in the school of prayer". Schooldays imply progress and deepened understanding, and with these in view involve discipline and application.

Paul here speaks of "continuing instant" in prayer. The verb suggests an attitude of devotion and indeed of determination. We give ourselves to prayer in that we are constantly asking, like the disciples, "Lord teach us to pray". We devote ourselves to the task with an awareness of our responsibility, as well as our privilege, of worshipping the Lord who is worthy of our adoration. It is prayer of this kind which Paul presents here as one of the instruments God gives us to help us to be "patient in tribulation". It is as we explore all the aspects of the prayer life that we discover what many of the great sufferers have found, that, in Cowper's words,

> "Prayer makes the darkened cloud withdraw,
> Prayer climbs the ladder Jacob saw,
> Gives exercise to faith and love,
> Brings every blessing from above."

Prayer begins in an adoring wonder as the realisation dawns on the soul that this One whom we approach is the sovereign ruler of the universe and He is also our Father. To bow in adoration is not only to adopt the only fitting attitude to our God, it is also to discover one more answer to our sufferings. A serious side-effect of our pains is that we easily become inward looking. We are taken up with our own crushing problems and, unless we are careful, self-pity will begin to dominate us. But to adore God is to be lifted outside ourselves. To bow in wonder before this transcendent majesty whose glory fills the heavens and whose mighty power spans the wide compass of history and reaches with unerring accuracy into every crevice of time and space, this is to mount up from a grovelling obsession with our own needs to an awe-inspiring glimpse of the glory of the eternal God. While Job fought with his problems and tried to find the answer in his own arguments he sank deeper into the morass of misery. It was when he began to contemplate the overwhelming majesty of God that he learnt to humble himself. It was in that self-abasement that he learnt a meek submission before God, and in that he also discovered, what his logic had failed to give, the peace of God which passes understanding.

Closely allied to adoration is praise. We praise God when our spirit responds with an inward song to what God has revealed about Himself. As we read the Scriptures we find God not only telling us about His mighty acts but explaining their significance as pointers to the kind of God He is. So too when we meet Him in the experiences of life, we discover that the truths of Scripture find an echo in our own living. He is gracious and kind, good and merciful, patient and forbearing. So we praise Him for the wonder of His being what He is. Again, it is true that while praise is primarily directed Godwards, and must never be viewed as a means to an end, the end being our comfort, yet none the less it does affect us in our pains. To learn to praise God constantly is to discover the transforming power of praise, for the very pain which has so filled our mind with perplexity or fear or anxiety is transmuted into one more occasion for praising God.

Praise and thanksgiving are closely linked. Thanksgiving is specific and detailed. We enumerate the benefits that we have received. We stir up our memory to furnish forgotten illustrations of the goodness of God. We trace His providence in our lives and from His guidance discover fresh grounds for thanking Him. But thanksgiving tends to crowd out less worthy thoughts. The querulous attitude in which we complain to God about our trials capitulates in face of the determined resolve to dwell on our blessings and to cultivate a grateful heart. William Cowper again put it so well,

"Have you no words? Ah think again,
Words flow apace when you complain,
And fill your fellow creature's ear
With the sad tale of all your care.

Were half the breath thus vainly spent,
To heaven in supplication sent,
Your cheerful song would oftener be –
Hear what the Lord has done for me!"

Our complaining also dies when we begin to confess our sins. At the hub of true prayer is a continuing spirit of penitence. How could it be otherwise? I cannot contemplate the glory of God and His great love to me without being made aware of my own sin. Nor is it simply the sins of commission in which by word and deed I have displeased Him, which are my troubled concern. There are

130

the sins of omission – the coldness of heart which has not responded to His gracious love, the ingratitude which has received benefits beyond reckoning and has so often taken them for granted, the lack of concern for God's honour, the lukewarmness in service. All these and other lacks beside make us confess, "We have left undone those things which we ought to have done; and we have done those things which we ought not to have done."

But confession and complaint cannot live together. How can I remonstrate with God about what I judge to be His failure to spare me pain when there is so much in my life which is crying to heaven for His rebuke and His chastening? How dare I take God to task for His unreadiness to give me a comfortable existence when there are so many counts on which I myself have to answer? Indeed, as my awareness of my sinful failure grows, I am forced to the Psalmist's admission, "He has not dealt with us after our sins nor rewarded us according to our iniquities" (Ps. 103: 10). Had He done so we would have perished, but instead He has been merciful and has freely forgiven. So confession of sin distils into the joyful realisation of God's pardon and we are back in the realm of praise. But in this transition our own self-centred attitudes are engulfed by a new awareness of God.

Prayer is also aspiration. We are content yet never content, satisfied yet always dissatisfied. This is the paradox, that we rejoice in God and yet press on to have further cause to rejoice. We are satisfied in our souls yet we hunger and thirst for more. This aspiration is summed up in the Psalmist's cry, "My heart and my flesh cry out for the living God" (Ps. 42: 2). It is heard again in Paul's prayer, "That I may know Him" (Ph. 3: 10). But every advance in the knowledge of God brings healing to the troubled soul. To know Him as my Father is to learn more of His loving care. To know Christ as my Saviour is to grow in my understanding of His rich sympathy. To seek for the Holy Spirit is to discover why the chastening comes; it is part of His gracious activity as He refines, purifies and makes holy. So aspiration after God not only draws us out after Him, it is also a blessing to us in our pains, as it turns our thoughts from our suffering to seek Him with all our heart.

Prayer is of course asking. I put it last not because it is unimportant but because it emerges from what has gone before, and because we too often reverse the order and put asking first. As a result we often fail to worship and praise and seek after God Himself. Yet intercession is an integral part of prayer, and, like every other element in prayer, it turns us out from ourselves. We not only pray specifically for our own needs but for the needs of others. Nor do we pray only for a narrow circle but for men and women across the world. To mature in the ministry of prayer is to widen our horizons more and more, as new people and fresh needs are brought to mind by the prompting of the Spirit.

It is at this point that the question often arises: "Should I not pray for healing in times of sickness, whether for myself or for others?" Indeed some would go further and frame the question more insistently: "Should I not act in faith and claim healing from the Lord?" The reply from other Christians may be very different: "Yes, you may pray for God's blessing on the medical means used, and you may ask Him that if it is His will, He would heal you. But you have no right to expect a miraculous cure." Here are the two opposing positions with one side confining such miracles to the apostolic era, and the other insisting that it is only lack of faith which shuts us out from seeing such miracles today.

The issues raised by this debate are too far-reaching to be dealt with in one short chapter. Indeed they would require an additional book. However, at the risk of appearing to examine a major issue in a brief and cursory fashion, some observations must be made. To those who refuse the reality of miraculous healing today one need only point to clear examples of genuine healing which are not to be denied simply because there have been false claims based on faulty diagnosis, temporary alleviation or psychological manipulation. We dare not impose limits on the sovereign freedom of God Almighty unless He has given us a clear and unambiguous mandate for such a restriction. On the other side of the debate those who claim that the Christian should never be ill must face the clear evidence of the New Testament. While the Apostles saw very many miracles of healing, they did not always exercise the power to heal. So Paul prescribes medicine for Timothy's chronic stomach trouble (1 Ti. 5: 23), he leaves Trophimus sick at Miletus (2 Ti. 4: 20) and he himself had to live with his thorn in the flesh.

Such clear evidence precludes the use of Matthew 8: 17 to claim that healing is "in the atonement" in the sense that we should therefore expect to be free from sickness. It is true that the sicknesses which He bore were the evidence of divine judgement on a sinful race, and the sympathy which He showed in His healing ministry reached its climax in His suffering on the cross when He bore the sin which lies behind the sicknesses. His atonement has given us freedom from the guilt and power of sin, but there is no promise of freedom from the presence of sin in this world – sinless perfection has no place in the gospel. The atonement which deals with our sins is certainly the pledge of heaven in which not only sin but the consequences of sin, sickness and death, will be banished. It also means that even now the real sting of sickness and death is drawn for the believer, for they are no longer the heralds of coming doom. However, all this does not mean that sickness will be totally banished from our bodies in this world any more than we can expect to check the onset of death by the power of faith. We may therefore pray to God for healing whether in the use of medical means or by His direct action. There may be times when He will grant the gift of faith which will enable us to pray for healing with confident assurance and indeed with boldness (Ja. 5: 15). But there will be other times when we will be given grace to say "Not my will but thine be done". We must never infringe God's sovereign discretion whether to grant healing or the grace to endure. To go further, as some do, and accuse a sufferer of lack of faith, or what is possibly even worse, to imply that one who has lost a loved one did not exercise faith, is not only to add pain in an utterly insensitive way, but to draw a completely unwarranted conclusion from Scripture.

Intercession is essentially outward looking. Yet once again it is true that the more we give ourselves to concern for others, the more we are enriched ourselves. The principle of Proverbs 11: 24 still applies, "There is that scattereth and yet increaseth; and there is that withholdeth more than is meet, but it tendeth to poverty." So too Ecclesiastes, the preacher, urges us, "Cast thy bread upon the waters: for thou shall find it after many days" (Ec. 11: 1). We do not pray for others in order to benefit ourselves, but in God's economy there is precisely this result. As we pray for others' needs we begin to see our own problems in a new light. As we plead before God for the lonely suffering of an imprisoned Christian in some communist prison cell we begin to reflect on our own favoured state. Some of the great intercessors have proved this. The hands which turned the leaves of the prayer list may have been grotesquely twisted with pain, their prayer times may have been sleepless nights, their sanctuary may have been the terminal ward of a hospital, yet there they have prayed, and not only has many a missionary felt the impact of their praying, but they themselves have been blessed. Often without being themselves consciously aware of it, they have been transformed from being what they might have been, querulous sufferers, to what in fact they have become, joyful combatants in the front rank of the church militant.

Rejoicing in hope, continuing steadfastly in prayer – here is the way, under God, to persist in face of suffering. An illustration may perhaps help. Before the advent of tractors a familiar feature of the countryside was the ploughman with his two heavy horses pulling the plough. The ground might be rough, but the ploughshare was sharp and cut through the soil. Yet it was not only the sharpness of the share which was needed, but the united strength of the two horses pulling steadily side by side under the skilled hands of the ploughman. Pain and suffering can produce very rough ground indeed, yet the sharp ploughshare of persistence will cut through the roughest terrain if the hand of faith holds firmly to the united power of hope and prayer. To rejoice in the hope of glory, to devote ourselves to prayer in all its richness, this is the way to face whatever pains may come and to endure to the end.

Let John Wesley have the final word in two verses from his translation of J. A. Rothe's German hymn – a hymn which provided comfort for Wesley's great and godly contemporary, Fletcher of Madeley, in his dying hours:

"Though waves and storms go o'er my head,
Though strength and health and friends be gone,
Though joy be withered all and dead,
Though every comfort be withdrawn,
On this my steadfast soul relies
Father, Thy mercy never dies.

Fixed on this ground will I remain,
Though my heart fail and flesh decay;
This anchor shall my soul sustain
When earth's foundations melt away;
Mercy's full power I then shall prove,
Loved with an everlasting love."